BIG PACIFIC

BIG PACIFIC

REBECCA TANSLEY

Princeton University Press
Princeton and Oxford

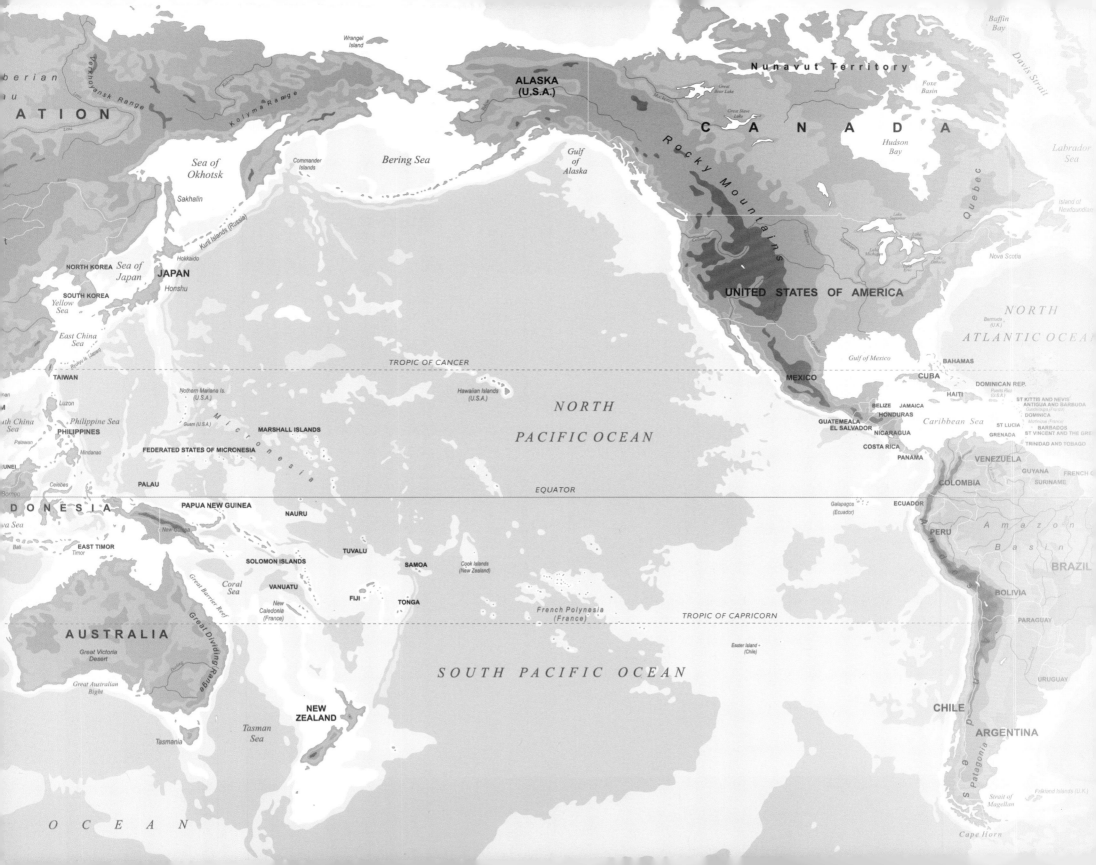

Contents

Big Pacific

Deepest. Widest. Largest. The Pacific attracts an ocean of superlatives – yet none of them really capture its unassailable immensity, startling diversity or sheer poetry of its ever-shifting nature. It defies definition.

Mere facts can describe its physical attributes. At 166 million square kilometers (64 million square miles), it covers one-third of the Earth's total surface area and accounts for nearly half of the planet's water surface – larger than all of the Earth's land area combined. We are all inhabitants of planet Pacific.

Hidden beneath its darkest waters is the deepest point on the planet, nearly 11 kilometers (7 miles) down. Even the Pacific's average depth – 4,280 meters (14,040 feet) – is astounding, putting estimates of its total water volume at more than 700 million cubic kilometers (168 million cubic miles). It is perhaps the closest thing to boundless that we know.

Yet limits it has. Touching most of the world's continents, and dotted by archipelagoes, the Pacific has enticed people to brave its expanse for millennia. It has been a frontier to explore, a space to conquer, a resource to plunder – and a place of infinite wonder.

No doubt it had many names before the one it bears now, gifted to it in 1520 by Portuguese navigator Ferdinand Magellan and belied ever since by both its volatile nature and violent history. For even on its calmest day the Pacific is anything but a peaceful ocean.

Passionate, mysterious, violent and voracious, the Pacific is the world's largest stage for nature's unending drama – one in which we humans play an increasingly major part.

The sea is only the embodiment of the supernatural and wonderful existence. It is nothing but love and emotion; it is the "Living Infinite." — Jules Verne

Passionate
Pacific

The eternal quest to multiply has driven life in the Pacific into a stunning array of unusual behaviors and adaptations — all designed to propel each species into the future.

FROM AWE AND AVARICE to war and wanderlust — the Pacific Ocean has attracted every passion ever experienced by humankind. It has been the focus of our fascination for as long as we have lived around and in it, and we will continue to love and learn from it well into the future.

Perhaps its vast, life-giving body speaks to our own primordial origins within its embrace. Perhaps we respond to an innately human need to understand its place on our planet. Or we marvel at its capacity to create and sustain a seemingly infinite variety of life – including our own. Whatever the reason for our enchantment, there is no doubt the Pacific holds a place in our hearts. Driven by this passion, we explore its remotest reaches, harvest its bounty and delve into its myriad mysteries.

Much of its allure lies with the creatures that inhabit it, from the mammals, birds, fish and invertebrates that populate its shores and shallows to the enigmatic species that thrive in its depths. But these animals demonstrate their own remarkable passion for life: the enduring commitment of a mate to its partner, the selfless devotion of a parent to its offspring, the all-consuming but doomed drive to procreate. These passions are an inexorable part of life in the Pacific, each one an everyday miracle in its own way – and an integral part of the passionate force of nature that is the Big Pacific.

◀ As far as inter-species relationships are concerned, that of a clownfish and the sea anemone it calls home is one of the most fascinating.

Great white wanderers

Peripatetic pilgrims of the Pacific, **Great white sharks** have one of the widest geographic ranges of any marine animal. Individuals migrate vast distances – even across entire ocean basins – and in the Pacific they can be found as far north as Alaska and as far south as New Zealand's Sub-Antarctic Islands.

Every year, however, a great many of these oceanic travelers congregate around La Isla Guadalupe (Guadalupe Island), 241 kilometers (150 miles) off the western coast of Mexico. First to arrive, in spring and summer, are males. The females – who generally dwarf the males – arrive in the fall. It's thought mating occurs in the late fall, although no one has ever witnessed great whites in the act.

Pregnant females spend a year or more at sea while as many as ten embryos develop inside their bodies. At birth the pups measure around a meter (3 to 4 feet). Like their parents, these youngsters disappear into the deep blue, perhaps using their remarkable ability to read the magnetic fields of the Earth's crust to navigate their way across the ocean.

UNITED STATES

Los Angeles

Guadalupe Is. ✪

MEXICO

Mexico City

▶ *Unlike most other fish, Great whites are endothermic, which means they can maintain parts of their body at temperatures above that of the surrounding water. This enables them to survive in sub-temperate as well as temperate and tropical seas.*

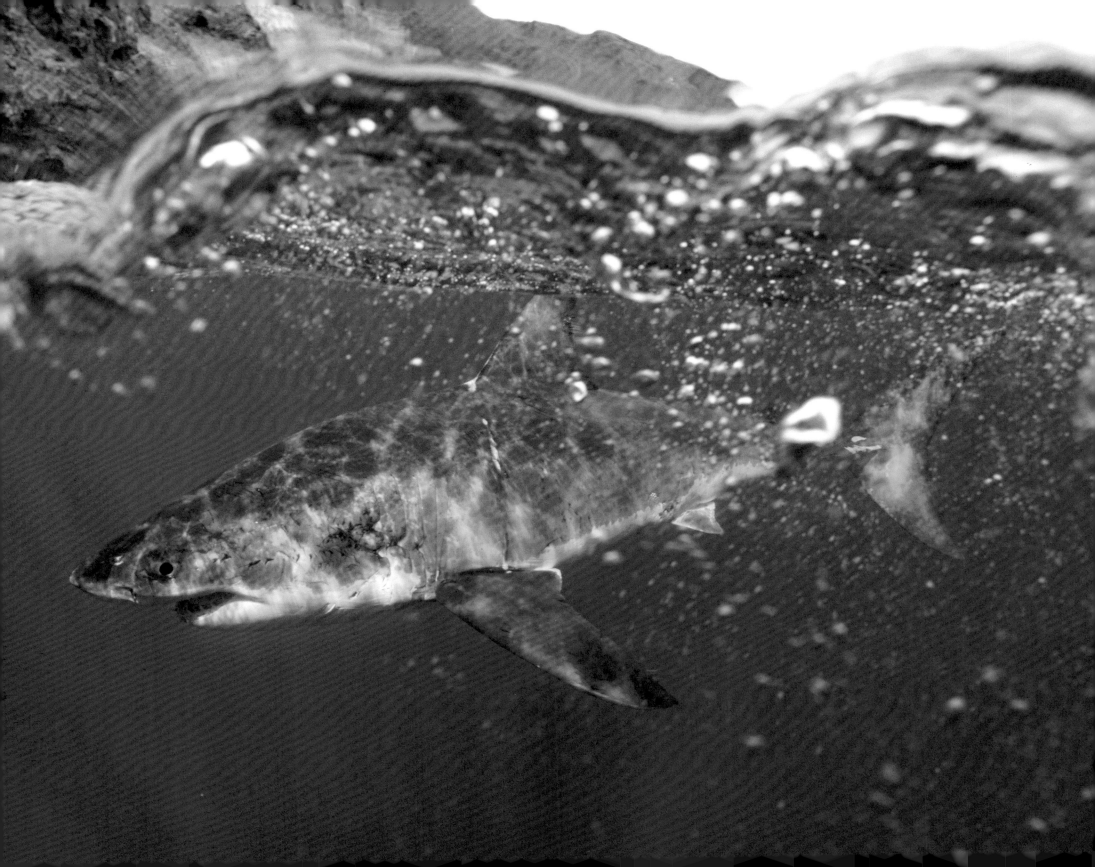

▶ With little obvious differentiation other than the size disparity, it can be tricky to distinguish between male and female Great whites. Males, however, have 'claspers' – twin organs broadly equivalent to a penis with which they inseminate females during mating. The claspers on this male Great white shark can be seen to the left of the pelvic fin. A researchers' tag is visible on the shark's side.

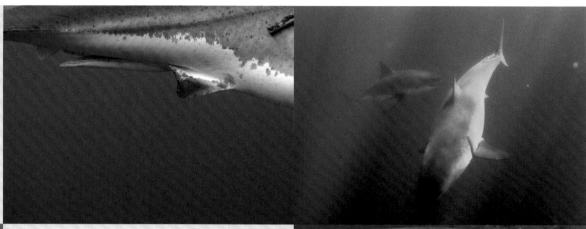

◀ Bite marks commonly seen on the heads of females at Guadalupe suggest mating is a vigorous encounter, with the male likely using his impressive array of teeth to maintain a grip on his larger, stronger partner.

▶ Shark cage diving enables adventurous – and not-so-adventurous – tourists to observe the world's largest predatory fish from the relative safety of an aluminum frame. The activity is becoming common in areas Great whites are known to frequent, such as Guadalupe Island, southern New Zealand and, right, Port Lincoln, Australia.

▲ Unsurprisingly for such a highly evolved predator, Great white sharks are endowed with keen sensory organs. Their sense of smell – which enables them to detect a single drop of blood in 10 billion drops of water – is legendary and helps give rise to their fearsome reputation as hunters. But their vision is also good: the retina of a Great white's eye is dually adapted for day vision and low light. Even more impressive is their ability to detect electrical currents through pores on their snouts which are filled with cells called the ampullae of Lorenzini.

Great white sharks

Like many terrestrial apex predators, the Great white shark has suffered significant population decline. The species was officially protected by South Africa in 1991, by California in 1994 and by New Zealand in 2007.

Seals at the seashore

The waters around Guadalupe Island are abundant in prey species for the Great white shark. Both **Northern elephant seals** and **Guadalupe fur seals** breed here, and pups of both species – unaware of the local hazards lurking just offshore – make an easy meal for an apex predator.

The elephant seals like to lounge along the island's beaches, while the smaller fur seals frequent the rocky coastline. Adult members of both species must head out to sea to hunt, however, leaving their pups behind to play in the shallows. This is when youngsters are most vulnerable to the sharks.

Northern elephant seals are the second largest true seal. Females grow up to 3 meters (10 feet) in length and weigh as much as 600 kilograms (1,300 pounds), but the gargantuan males can measure 4 meters (13 feet) or more and tip the scales at more than 2,000 kilograms (5,000 pounds).

These super-sized marine mammals have adapted well to their sunbathing habits. Their noses actually act like 're-breathers' that re-absorb moisture when the animals exhale, minimizing the loss of water when they are hauled out on land.

▶ *Northern elephant seals bask in the Guadalupe sun.*

◀ *An elephant seal's whiskers or vibrissae are thought to assist in the detection of prey.*

Fur seals, elephant seals

Hunted to near extinction in the eighteenth and nineteenth centuries, the Guadalupe fur seal has made an encouraging comeback. Similarly Northern elephant seals, once much in demand for oil and blubber, were considered extinct by the late 1800s. However, a remnant population was discovered on Guadalupe Island and the Mexican government enforced protection in 1922. Thanks to this measure, every elephant seal on the North American mainland is today a descendant of the Guadalupe survivors.

▶ *Northern elephant seals belong to the Phocidae family of 'earless' seals so are regarded as 'true' seals, while their Guadalupe neighbors, the fur seals, are not because they have visible ear flaps. In the photo below left the 'earless' elephant seal can be seen on the left, while the ear flap is clearly visible on the fur seal on the right.*

Spawning spectacle

Mysteriously driven by the moon's cycle, the mass spawning of **Palolo worms** leads to a unique annual harvest on many Pacific islands. In Samoa it is an eagerly anticipated, communal event.

Equidistant between Hawai'i and New Zealand, Samoa is part of the group of islands known as Polynesia. Samoans have long been sustained by the Pacific's bounty, and they regard the protein-rich Palolo worms as an extra-special gift of the sea.

Once a year, groups of islanders flock to the shore and, with nets, buckets and flashlights at the ready, wade into the water to await the arrival of the worms.

◀ *Just before dawn the spawning of the Palolo worms begins. Local people head to the coast, armed with torches, to harvest this bounty.*

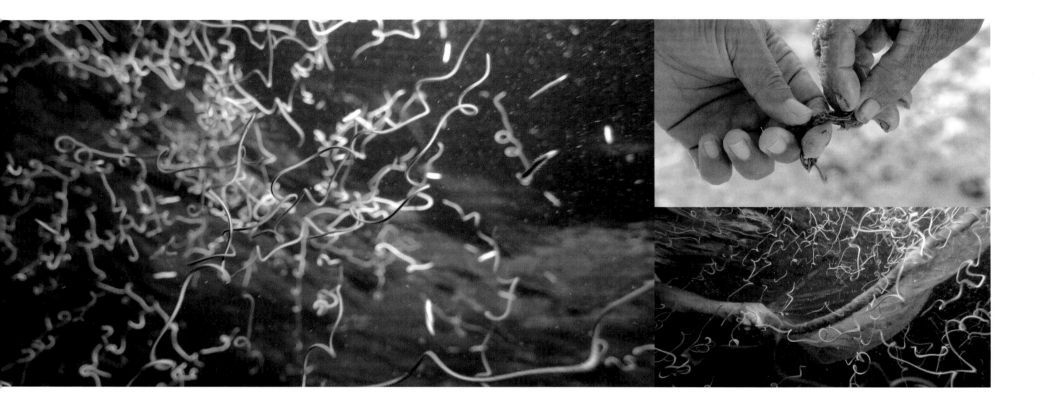

▲ *Harvested epitokes are eaten raw, fried in butter or cooked with egg or onion.*

▶ *A lone watcher awaits the emergence of the Palolo worm.*

Between midnight and dawn – the timing depends on the exact location – the first few worms emerge from the coral reefs. Soon their writhing forms swirl upwards in the water like a frenzy of animated scribbles.

For the people of Samoa and other Pacific islands where Palolo are harvested, this unusual event leads to a traditional gastronomic treat. For the Palolo worms, however, it has even greater significance.

Measuring around 30 centimeters (12 inches) in length, these animals spend most of their lives buried inside the substrate of the ocean floor. Once a year they undergo a remarkable transformation, sprouting an extended tail segment, called an epitoke, that is filled with either eggs or

sperm. The epitoke – colored either pale tan (male) or blue-green (female) – also sports a primitive, light-sensitive eye that guides it to the sea's surface.

Prompted somehow by lunar phases, all the worms in one area release their epitokes more or less in unison. This simultaneous timing maximizes the chances of fertilization and creates one of the ocean's greatest mass spawning events.

With so many eggs and sperm released in close proximity, the sea becomes a milky, gelatinous soup. After fertilization, the eggs drift away on the currents to hatch into larvae. For a time these form part of the ocean's planktonic biomass, but eventually the maturing worms settle on the seafloor to begin the miraculous and mysterious cycle again.

Clowning around

The bond between a **clownfish** and its sea anemone host is one of the Pacific's most endearing partnerships. Clownfish are even commonly referred to as anemone fish, so strongly are they associated with their invertebrate pals.

There are 30 species of clownfish, each sporting its own combination of striking markings. They all live in the shallow waters of sheltered reefs or lagoons, and all display the same passion for anemones, forging with them a relationship that gives new meaning to the term 'codependency'.

The contract between vertebrate and invertebrate is relatively simple. An anemone may host up to a dozen members of the same species at any time, providing its fishy friends with a safe haven from predators and a sheltered nesting place. In return, the clownfish rid their anemone of parasites and help circulate water around its tentacles – effectively delivering it food.

▶ *Clownfish live in a hierarchical community within the reach of any one of many types of sea anemone.*

Nature cleverly endows clownfish with a mucus-like covering which protects them from their host's venomous sting. However, acclimation must occur for the clownfish to become immune. To achieve this, the clownfish swims around and through the anemone, rubbing its ventral side and fins on the tentacles.

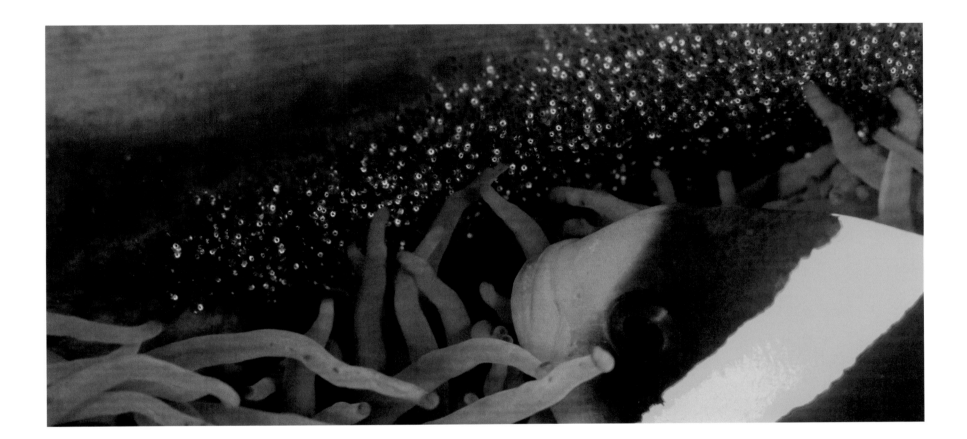

This may seem a marriage of convenience, but the symbiosis is so strong that a clownfish may not survive if separated from its anemone. So – understandably – clownfish are extremely territorial. They can live for up to ten years, and during this time they never stray far from their 'home'.

In a strange quirk of nature, all clownfish are born male, and only the most dominant member of the colony will develop into a female. The newly minted female holds all the reproductive rights and the rest of the group adheres to a strict hierarchy under her rule. Only one fish – selected by the 'queen' – is able to mate with her. All the other clownfish remain unable to reproduce, although just how the dominant pair is able to suppress the development of the remaining members of the group remains a mystery.

Female clownfish spawn roughly every two weeks, laying hundreds of eggs at a time. The favored male then fertilizes them and faithfully guards them around the clock, constantly fanning them with his fins. After ten days the eggs hatch and the larvae drift towards the sea surface. They return to their reef as juveniles, following the scent of the anemone that was imprinted upon them at birth.

▲ *Sheltered in the arms of the anemone, a male clownfish tends a cluster of eggs by circulating water, oxygenating the eggs and providing fresh food for the anemone at the same time.*

Clownfish are small – typically growing to no more than 11 centimeters (4½ inches) in length.

Family affair

The **Yellow-eyed penguin** is one of the world's rarest penguins. Equally dependent on land and sea, it is – unusually for a penguin – not a colonial bird, instead breeding in pairs in temperate coastal forests, scrubland and cliffs.

Yellow-eyed penguins are model parents. They mate for life, working together to build a shallow nest of twigs, grass and leaves, often in the tangled roots of trees. The female typically lays a single clutch of two eggs, which both birds take turns incubating for up to 51 days. This division of labor continues after the chicks hatch, when one parent will return to sea to feed while the other stays on duty with the youngsters. Despite such devoted parenting, only 18 of 100 penguin chicks survive their first year of life due to predation, disease and human disturbance.

Although they appear keen-eyed, the birds are short-sighted on land, as their vision is adapted for underwater conditions. When foraging at sea they may travel as far as 25 kilometers (15 miles) from land and dive to depths of 120 meters (400 feet) in search of small to medium-sized fish, squid and crustaceans.

▲ *Throughout the summer Yellow-eyed penguin chicks are always under the watchful eye of one of their two parents.*

On its return to the nest, a Yellow-eyed penguin parent releases the other parent from the role of caregiver before being urged to 'cough up' a meal for the hungry chicks.

◄ *The Yellow-eyed penguin habitat lies within the Roaring Forties – a band of ocean below the 40th parallel south where large tracts of uninterrupted ocean allow high winds to develop. Returning to shore often involves negotiating tumultuous seas, after which the birds face a lengthy inland walk over rocks and through pastureland and forest to reach their nesting site.*

Yellow-eyed penguins

Once widespread along much of New Zealand's Pacific coastline, the Yellow-eyed penguin population has been ravaged by introduced carnivores from which they have little protection, and has been negatively affected by habitat loss and human disturbance. Today, only wild areas in the remote South-east of New Zealand offer hope for the endangered birds' continued existence on the mainland. Their survival rests on the eradication of pests such as feral cats, ferrets and stoats, and careful management of human impact.

Marine monogamists

Beneath the green waters of coastal British Columbia, one species sets the bar for enduring long-term relationships. The **Wolf eel** – actually a type of fish called a blenny, rather than a true eel – lives out its entire life with its chosen mate, even remaining single for the rest of its life when its partner dies.

Here in the Pacific's Northeast, the sea is cold, with an average annual water temperature of around 10° Celsius (48 to 50° Fahrenheit). Cold water is richer in oxygen and this gives the entire food chain a boost, leading to larger – albeit slower-growing – organisms. The Wolf eel is no exception to this rule;

▲ *Wolf eels move through the water by making deep S-shapes with their bodies, like a snake. Their large heads and fierce-looking mouths make them appear dangerous, but they are only aggressive towards other Wolf eels.*

▲ A fiercely protective mother, the female coils herself around her brood, settling the eggs into a spherical cluster, before the male coils around her in his own shielding embrace.

it can grow up to 2.5 meters (8 feet) in length, weigh up to 40 kilograms (88 pounds) and live for more than 30 years, most of it spent tucked away in a rocky crevice with its partner.

Female Wolf eels settle down with their chosen mates at around seven years of age, when they will lay up to 10,000 eggs at a time. Once hatched, Wolf eel larvae leave their parents' lair to drift in sea currents. Juvenile Wolf eels spend their early lives in the mid-depths of the open ocean, but as they mature they head to shallower water. Eventually they find a mate and a den, and spend the rest of their lives together in the security of their home, emerging only to hunt for prey.

The jaws of a Wolf eel are very strong, enabling them to crush the shells of the crustaceans that make up the bulk of their diet. The conical, fang-like teeth of this male Wolf eel grip the crab, while strong back molars will pulverize its shell. Sadly, the fate of many Wolf eels is often slow starvation, for the tough armor of their prey gradually wears down their teeth, eventually rendering the eels unable to eat.

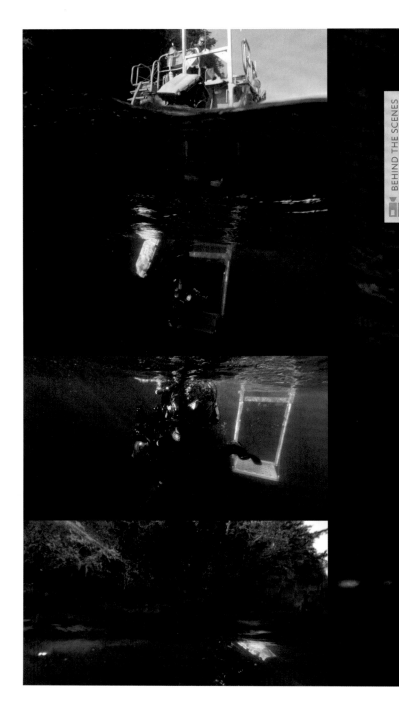

Elevator pitch

Capturing the dedication of Wolf eels to each other and to their brood of eggs entailed long hours underwater for Big Pacific Director of Photography Peter Kragh. But staying submerged for any amount of time in water of 6 or 7° Celsius (42 to 44° Fahrenheit) requires careful preparation – and a lot of extra equipment.

To extend dive time Kragh utilized a re-breather, an apparatus that absorbs a diver's exhaled carbon dioxide so the diver can access the unused oxygen content of each breath. But this doesn't solve the fundamental problem of staying warm. To do that, Kragh wore a drysuit, and beneath that a battery-operated heated suit – a bit like an electric blanket for his torso – which he turned on and off intermittently as required, primarily to keep his hands functioning.

If that sounds cozy, consider that this extra equipment – together with the camera and additional weights required to offset the buoyancy of the drysuit – added an extra 80 kilograms (180 pounds) of gear that Kragh had to wear. While diving this isn't such an issue, but it sure is when getting into and climbing out of often rough water. So a dive boat with a custom-built elevator that could lower him into and raise him out of the water proved an innovation that, for Kragh, was love at first sight.

"Up in British Columbia it's cold, it's often rough and it's often rainy. Anything you can do to be more productive in that environment is great."

Many-armed mollusks

With their bizarre form, intelligent behavior and mastery of the art of disguise, octopuses have long fascinated us. They may seem in a class of their own, but officially they are mollusks. This means they are invertebrates, because they have no internal or external skeleton, and it can be helpful to consider them an 'inside-out' mollusk in which the soft body is exposed and the shell has been reduced to two small plates onto which the head muscles are anchored.

Developing in the cold coastal waters of the northern Pacific, the Giant Pacific octopus can weigh twice as much as the average human and stretch more than 7 meters (25 feet) from tentacle tip to tentacle tip – although one specimen

▶ *The eight arms of an octopus (this animal is missing two) are covered with powerful suction cups. These chitin-ringed disks power the octopus's sense of touch and taste and endow them with an uncanny ability to cling onto almost any surface.*

The Giant Pacific Octopus is a stealthy predator, using the element of surprise and a burst of speed to snaffle an unsuspecting crab. Once the octopus snares its prey, it pulls it apart with its strong arms or beak, or drills a hole through the shell to inject its toxin. This paralyzes the prey and dissolves the connective tissue that attaches the animal's flesh to its shell, making it easier for the octopus to eat. The octopus returns to its den for a leisurely meal, after which it discards the shell into a garbage pile, or midden, just outside the lair.

◄ *This 8-centimeter (3-inch) octopus is known as the Larger Pacific striped octopus and is so recently discovered that at the time of publication there is no scientific name.*

stretched 9.1 meters (29 feet) across and weighed more than 272 kilograms (600 pounds).

The Pacific Ocean is home to many different species of octopus. These include the world's largest, the **Giant Pacific octopus,** and the very latest species to be discovered, the enigmatic **Larger Pacific striped octopus.**

The Larger Pacific striped octopus was only recently revealed as a resident of the Pacific coastal waters of Central America. In many ways it is similar to other better-known octopi – its skin flashes and ripples with the color changes typically associated with these masters of disguise – but its mating behavior is strikingly unique.

Unlike most other octopus mating rituals, in which the male briefly inserts a sperm-laden arm into the female's oviduct, female Larger Pacific striped octopus envelop males in a lengthy embrace that may last hours. The male curls his special appendage into position inside the female's mantle, but in return the female snakes an arm around his mantle and tightens her grip into a stranglehold.

Also unlike many other octopus, female Larger Pacific striped octopuses don't die after laying their eggs, instead going on to lay again and again. The females meticulously tend their eggs, jetting water over them with their siphons to keep them healthy with oxygenated water and regularly cleaning them to remove bacteria and algae. Once the larvae are mature, the mother triggers their hatching with her siphon.

▲ The tiny Blue-ringed octopus may be shy but its bite is power-packed with a lethal cocktail that makes it the only octopus species capable of killing a human.

A female Larger Pacific striped octopus finds a suitable place to lay her eggs. Here she guards them devotedly, cleaning and aerating them. When the larvae are ready, she triggers their hatching. Escaping the egg sacs is a challenge. The baby octopuses must coil and stretch themselves to squeeze out of their natal shells. Then, newly independent, the tiny aquanauts must brave an ocean full of predators. Those that survive eventually sink to the seafloor to take up residence and renew the cycle of octopus life.

▶ Dugongs are model mothers. After a long gestation of thirteen to fourteen months, they give birth to a single calf that they will nurse for eighteen months or more. A calf will remain with its mother for up to seven years while it learns to feed and contend with predators. Dugong dads, on the other hand, are far from the fatherly type. Extremely territorial, they court females that come into their range assiduously but play no role in raising the calf.

▲ The flukes and forelimbs of a Dugong are similar to those of dolphins, but the front flippers can also be used to 'walk' along the seabed or push off from it.

Mermaid moms

The word **'dugong'** originates from the Tagalog word for 'lady of the sea', and while the marine mammals that carry this name may not match the traditional western image of a mermaid, they certainly evince a beguiling, serene nature.

Found throughout the warm waters of the Pacific's tropical west, Dugongs are the only entirely vegetarian marine mammal, which gives rise to their other nickname of 'sea cow'. Their grazing habits lend them the un-mermaid-like appearance of living vacuum cleaners for, using their muscular snout with its large sensitive bristles, they forage for sea grass on the seafloor, suctioning it up roots and all.

Dugongs are highly social animals and are typically found in large herds. They communicate, much like dolphins, with chirps, whistles and barks. Their sense of smell is acute – it is thought they can distinguish aquatic plants at considerable distances. Sensory bristles all over their bodies, and in particular on their snout, help them pick up vibrations in the surrounding water.

Much shyer than their Atlantic cousin, the Manatee, Dugongs may look ponderous and slow but are capable of bursts of speed, and long, deep dives. They are known to travel great distances in search of a particular field of sea grass, but on the other hand may remain in one range for most of their lives. The sheer size of most adults – up to 4 meters (13 feet) affords them protection from predators such as sharks and crocodiles, but young Dugongs depend on their mothers for safety.

Dugongs

With a lifespan of 70 years or more and slow rate of reproduction, the Dugong is especially vulnerable to extinction. Dugongs have long been hunted by indigenous peoples in the areas where they are found, but modern human activity such as gill and mesh net fishing, shipping and habitat loss has exacerbated their population decline alarmingly. The species is officially classified as 'vulnerable to extinction' by IUCN and listed on CITES.

Human perils

Big Pacific Director of Photography Scott Snider experienced first hand one of the menaces threatening the Pacific while filming Dugong in the Philippines.

Dugongs are shy animals and their numbers are rapidly diminishing cue to unregulated hunting. Having finally located a mother and her calf, Snider and his safety diver were snorkeling towards them when a deafening underwater noise blasted through their bodies.

"We looked at each other," Snider remembers, "and shot back to our boat."

As Snider and his colleague suspected, the boom that rocked them had been a dynamite blast. In many parts of South East Asia the explosive is used – illegally – as a crude means of fishing, as it instantly kills or stuns large numbers of fish. The practice is highly destructive to the marine ecosystem, because the blasts are indiscriminate: they not only kill the few target fish, but also all other fish in the vicinity, large and small, the reef, and everything else in the area.

Back on board the boat, the crew's guide revealed he was also an auxiliary coastguard, and the men set off to locate the perpetrators of this damaging and dangerous practice. The culprits eluded apprehension, but the results of their work proved – sadly – easier to find. Snider and his colleague witnessed first hand the devastation wrought by the dynamite in what he describes as "the most depressing dive of my life."

"I have never seen anything like it and I wasn't prepared. Beautiful reef fish were lying dead everywhere, just littering the ground by the thousands. Even worse were the stunned fish, spinning and swirling in the water, trying in vain to reorient themselves. A pufferfish was swimming into a wall of coral and getting nowhere. Neon blue damsel fish struggled to stay buoyant above dozens of their kind that didn't make it. Heniochus butterfly, small Titan triggerfish,

and Leopard wrasse lay in the sand, gills pulsing rapidly as they waited to die. It was unbelievably wasteful and such a short-sighted way to get a few goat fish."

Snider explains that not all blast damage is instant, as the shock waves are also detrimental to coral tissue. Much of the hard and soft coral in the blast area was intact and looked normal, but in the coming days the tissue damage and resulting dead coral becomes obvious.

The only good news was that the Dugong mother and calf appeared unharmed, despite grazing just half a mile or so from the blast site. For Snider the experience was a sobering reminder of the threats facing the Big Pacific every day.

Conserving Pacific coral

Corals are some of Earth's most primitive animals, but also among the most ecologically important. Coral reefs foster the ocean's highest levels of biodiversity, supporting a quarter of all marine species by providing food and shelter for myriad fishes and invertebrates. They also protect coastlines from the destructive forces of storms and typhoons. In short, they play a vital role in the overall health of our planet.

Unfortunately corals are also fragile organisms – even those that produce hard, calcium-carbonate skeletons – and so are highly susceptible to environmental degradation and destructive fishing practices. They are also incredibly slow-growing: it can take 10,000 years for coral polyps to form a reef, and many more hundreds of years for the reef ecosystem to reach maturity.

Playing 'Mother Nature' with extremely slow-growing animals is a complicated, time-consuming endeavor, but corals do have one biological advantage that assists: they reproduce asexually, essentially cloning themselves. If a small piece of coral breaks off, it may settle, grow, and propagate. It is hoped that this special ability, known as fragmentation, can be used to enhance coral populations in areas that desperately need it.

This reef-rebuilding method has been successful in the Caribbean Sea, but conditions in this part of the Pacific Ocean can be considerably different. Every year, typhoons tear through the region – and one moderate storm could easily wipe out the fragile coral nurseries. The team's solution is to make the structures height-adjustable. This allows the baby corals to sit near the sunlit surface for most of their development, while ensuring they can be lowered to calmer depths when a storm approaches.

◀ *On Hainan Island near southern China the country's largest coral conservation project – a collaboration between the South China Sea Institute of Oceanology and the Nature Conservancy – has established a coral nursery, with the aim of re-building a reef.*

▶ First, an optimal location must be chosen as a nursery site. Corals require perfect conditions to grow – the right amount of sunlight, the correct water temperature, and adequate shelter from waves. Since the delicate pieces can't just be scattered around, structures for securing the coral fragments must be designed and built.

◀ Scientists carefully clip coral fragments from larger coral heads that have broken off. Each fragment is carefully attached to its nursery structure, just like decorating a Christmas tree. Then the waiting begins. It will take years before the coral fragments are robust enough to be transplanted onto reef locations.

When it's time to place the structures underwater, the team must anchor and buoy them simultaneously in place. The PVC reef frames must float at an optimal height for sunlight and nutrients to reach the new corals.

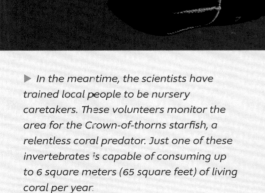

▶ In the meantime, the scientists have trained local people to be nursery caretakers. These volunteers monitor the area for the Crown-of-thorns starfish, a relentless coral predator. Just one of these invertebrates is capable of consuming up to 6 square meters (65 square feet) of living coral per year.

Coral reefs

Overfishing, ocean acidification, coastal development and climate change all impact on the health of coral reefs and the richly diverse ecosystems they sustain. Protecting them involves both responsible fishery management and habitat protection, but only a quarter of the world's reefs carry protected status. Organizations such as the The Nature Conservancy run coral remediation and restoration projects. Their success depends on continued resourcing and the willingness of people to respect the importance of coral reefs to our planet.

Coral reefs support diverse ecosystems in warm Pacific waters but they are threatened, not just by warming temperatures and ocean acidification but also by the plague-proportion outbreaks of the Crown-of-thorns starfish.

▲ Grunions grow up to about 20 centimeters (8 inches). They eat plankton, and are in turn an important prey species for many other fish, marine mammals and seabirds.

◀ Gulf grunions run their reproductive gauntlet during the day, while their Californian cousins – a closely related species – follow the same ritual at night.

Silver lightning

In the Gulf of California a strange tide follows the full moon, rushing towards an empty beach like quicksilver.

It begins as just a glimmer – a glint of silver in the breakers – but before long thousands of streamlined bodies swim defiantly through the shallows, heading directly for the beach. These are **Gulf grunions** and, in a rare event exclusive to this part of Mexico, they are embarking on one of the Pacific's strangest mating phenomena.

It begins with the flurry of silver bodies as shoals of females invade the beach. Here, like an army landing on D-Day, they dig in to the sand at the waves' furthest reach to lay their eggs. Before long the next wave of troops – the males – arrives. These soldiers, equally resolved, proceed to wrap themselves around the half-buried females and fertilize the eggs just laid.

The fish have just minutes to complete their passionate embrace and return to the ocean before they suffocate. By dusk the event is a memory, for as quickly as the silver mirage appeared, it vanishes.

◀ Surprisingly for so many fish out of water there are few mortalities; Grunions can survive for up to an hour out of the sea. But any stragglers are eagerly snapped up by seagulls and other shore birds. Seabirds, such as these Brown pelicans, also take advantage of the fish amassing in the shallows to pick up an easy lunch.

▶ The 'Grunion run' takes advantage of the high tides brought on by the full moon in spring and summer.

Once the female arrives on the sand she arches her body and excavates the semi-fluid sand with her tail to create a nest.

◀ In a desperate dance, she twists her body and digs into the sand until she is half buried, with her head sticking up. Here she deposits between 1,600 and 3,600 eggs. The tiny eggs sink and settle into the nest she has created.

The male wraps himself around the female to release 'milt' which flows down the female's body to fertilize the eggs. Up to eight males may fertilize the eggs in a single nest.

◀ The whole process only takes around 3 minutes. The fish return to the water as their place is taken by others.

▶ Turbulence generated by wave action buries the fertilized eggs under about 15 centimeters (5 inches) of moist sand. Here the fertilized embryos remain buried until the next spring tide when returning waters release the larvae.

▶ A female Tuatara lays her eggs inside a burrow selected for this process. Females lay between six and ten eggs every two to seven years. They do not remain with their brood, instead returning to their own burrow.

Absent parents

▲ While they may look like lizards, Tuatara are not members of the lizard family, although they are related. Physiological differences such as their skull structure and male reproductive organs distinguish them from many other reptiles.

▶ The crest of a Tuatara develops with adulthood, and that of males is typically more developed. Tuatara grow to between 30 and 75 centimeters (12 to 30 inches) long.

The story of the love life of the Tuatara is a short one, for the unique reptiles' courting and coupledom is as fleeting as the brush with parenthood that follows. Ironically, the brevity of their reproductive behavior is countered by their life expectancy which, in the absence of predators, is extremely long.

Indeed it appears that much in the life of the Tuatara happens slowly other than mating. The eggs, laid in shallow nests, require between 11 and 16 months of incubation, while the young take up to 13 years to attain sexual maturity. Tuatara commonly live 60 years or more, but may live a lot longer – perhaps up to a century or beyond.

Tuatara are territorial animals, so parents do not share a nest and their young receive no parenting at all. The solitary animals dig themselves burrows, or 'squat' in those made by a small seabird, the Fairy prion. These birds often create burrow complexes with interlocking tunnels and several entrances. This suits Tuatara, which can inhabit a section of the complex and take advantage of the small animals attracted to the birds' excreta as a kind of 'home-delivery' meal.

Often referred to as a 'living fossil', the Tuatara is a Rhynchocephalian reptile, the only surviving member of an order of which there were many other species some 200 million years ago when other dinosaurs roamed the Earth. Somehow the Tuatara survived extinction 60 million years ago and lived in New Zealand, unthreatened, until the arrival of humans.

A juvenile Tuatara snaffles up a spider on the forest floor. When older, the Tuatara will add small lizards, frogs and even baby birds to its diet.

Tuatara

Before the arrival of humans in New Zealand, the only predators of the Tuatara were large birds of prey. However, with the first wave of colonization of the country around 1250 to 1300AD came rats. Young Tuatara in particular were vulnerable to these pests. By the time European settlers arrived, bringing with them cats, dogs, ferrets, stoats and possums, the Tuatara was almost extinct on the mainland. Then those populations still surviving on offshore islands began to dwindle as mammalian predators invaded those havens too.

Today the Tuatara is now confined to offshore islands which are actively protected from predators, and it has been introduced into predator-free sanctuaries on the main islands. Pest extermination seems the only sure way to guarantee the survival of this unique animal in its homeland.

Paternal passion

In the temperate coastal waters of New Zealand, the largest seahorse in the world, the **Pot-bellied seahorse**, brings a whole new dimension to the concept of fatherhood.

These creatures, which have long charmed us with their prehensile tails and equine demeanor, live among seaweed and rocky reefs in intertidal and coastal waters. Here they feed on planktonic-sized crustaceans such as tiny shrimp, which they vacuum up from the water with their distinctive snouts.

▲ *Despite the fact that seahorse dads only ever carry the eggs of one female, seahorses have a reputation for promiscuity because they may dance with more than one partner during courtship. Scientists think this may be their way of checking out suitors for their next successful mating.*

▶ Pot-bellied seahorses engage in a ritualized courtship 'dance' that can last up to 20 minutes. To start, the male brightens his distended stomach pouch to a bright yellow hue and inflates and deflates it repeatedly. He then approaches his intended, head tucked down and tiny fins fluttering.

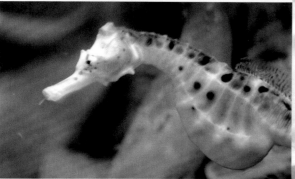

▲ Signaling her interest, the female rapidly enlivens her own usually discreet colors. Then, tails intertwined, the pair embark on an underwater 'pas de deux', pirouetting and mirroring each other. At some point, when they are belly to belly, the female squirts her eggs into the opening of the male's expanded pouch. Joined for but a brief moment, the pair then untangles and separates.

▶ Once 'pregnant,' the male's color dulls. The baby seahorses remain in his pouch after hatching to be safely incubated for around thirty days – depending on the water temperature. He then releases his brood before dawn, when up to 700 seahorse 'fry' float away on the tide.

Jewels of the sea

The protected Pacific seas around Palawan Island in the Philippines are home to the world's largest and rarest pearl-producing oyster, the **Golden pearl** or **Gold-lipped oyster**. As its name suggests, this mollusk produces a golden-hued pearl that is today one of the most coveted gems in the world.

Naturally occurring around Palawan, Gold-lipped oysters are notoriously sensitive in nature. Coaxing the perfect pearl from them is a highly involved and carefully managed process aimed at managing the many variables that can affect the oyster – and therefore the pearl within.

Pearls are formed when a tiny foreign particle finds its way into the living tissues of an oyster. The animal protects itself by coating the particle with layer upon layer of nacre – a type of calcium carbonate that is the same, light-reflecting substance that determines the color inside an oyster's shell.

THAILAND

CAMBODIA

VIETNAM

● *Manila*

PHILIPPINES

MALAYSIA

Palawan Island

▲ *The rare Gold-lipped oyster is now farmed in a process that has been perfected over time – to create the perfect pearl.*

▶ *Gold-lipped oysters are considered the giants of the oyster family, growing up to 30 centimeters (12 inches) in diameter.*

▲ The oysters spend three years on trays in the ocean as the pearl inside them slowly grows. During that time, they are carefully monitored and the surrounding water tested for pollutants.

Once only naturally occurring, wild pearls are now almost impossible to find, and every slight change in the ocean – temperature or nutrient levels, for example – affects the quality of the pearls they produce. Pearl farming now aims to exploit the natural process while controlling some of those variables to meet the world's passion for gems from the deep.

Cultured pearls are rounder and smoother than wild pearls, but there is never any guarantee of perfection, despite a rigorous five-year process. First, the farmers hand-raise Gold-lipped oyster babies – called 'spats' – for about two years, until they reach pearl-bearing size. With great precision, a miniscule piece of oyster shell is then delicately grafted inside the body of the oyster. This particle will form the nucleus of what will grow to be the world's only living gem.

Environmental conditions must be perfect for this alchemy to take place. The water temperature cannot fall below 29.5° Celsius (85° Fahrenheit) or above 31° Celsius (88° Fahrenheit)

or the oyster will die. The sea must be rich in oxygen and receive the right amount of sunlight to ensure sufficient plankton is present for the mollusk to eat. The current must be strong enough to deliver this to the oysters – but not so strong that they become stressed. The water must also be free of contaminants that can find their way into the oyster and affect the quality of its pearl.

The oysters – with their potential pearls – are then placed in trays in the ocean, where they are nurtured for an additional three years. Each oyster is monitored daily for signs of stress, while the surrounding water quality is tested for pollution. Predatory fish are chased away and the exterior shells of the oysters are meticulously cleaned of parasites and algae. All this time – five years – the developing pearl is invisible to its caretakers.

Finally, it is harvest time, when specially trained technicians patiently remove the new pearls, taking care not to harm the oysters. The pearls are then sorted, graded, and those rated close to perfect find their way to the highest-end markets.

Gold-lipped oyster

The first golden pearls produced in Palawan were cultured from some of the last remaining wild oysters. Now the Jewelmer farm at Palawan supports the species' survival. After producing several pearls the oysters from this farm are carefully returned to the ocean to spend the rest of their lives spawning naturally, helping to repopulate the Pacific Ocean with its golden treasure.

Consider the universal cannibalism of the sea; all whose creatures prey upon each other, carrying on eternal war since the world began. – HERMAN MELVILLE

Voracious
Pacific

There is plenty of food in the vastness of the ocean. The challenge to find that food drives all life in the Pacific. From the biggest to the smallest, every mouthful counts.

THE URGE TO SATISFY HUNGER is one of life's most basic impulses. It drives all animals – and some plants – to forage, harvest, hunt, ensnare or scavenge in countless different ways. This produces a diverse, often surprising array of behavior and, over time, helps to shape astounding adaptations.

Across the Pacific are many examples of the formative force of nature that is the need to eat: fish that leave the water, birds of flight that swim beneath the waves like fish. In an ironic twist, the biggest animals in the Pacific depend on the smallest for survival, and roam the ocean in search of them, while other creatures, anchored to one place, await the random offerings of the tide for fare which can outweigh them.

There are warm-blooded fish, thermodynamically propelled for bursts of pinpoint-accurate predatory speed, and monster jellyfish with mouths no bigger than a pinhead, simply adrift on oceanic currents.

In all their astonishing diversity these myriad organisms and appetites have one thing in common: their home, the vast, voracious Big Pacific.

▶ *The Whale shark is the world's biggest fish, with a mouth two meters (seven feet) across. Yet, like the world's largest mammal, the Blue whale, they are filter feeders, consuming plankton at an enormous rate.*

Behemoths of the blue

The open expanses of the Big Pacific are home to the largest animal ever known to have existed, the **Blue whale**. The weight-supporting qualities of water and the bounty of the sea have, together, enabled the evolution of this marine mammal into a gentle giant larger than any terrestrial animal could ever have grown. It is an evolutionary product of our ocean planet.

At birth a blue whale can measure up to 8 meters (25 feet) in length and weigh up to 2.7 tonnes (3 tons). Nourished solely by its mother's fat-rich milk for the first seven months of its life, it can grow up to 90 kilograms (200 pounds) a day so that, by adulthood, it stretches up to 30 meters (100 feet) in length, and weighs up to 200

tonnes (220 tons). Its heart is reputed to be the size of a small car – famously quipped to be a Volkswagen Beetle – although the comparison of such awe-inspiring natural creation with human invention does not, it can be argued, do this miraculous animal justice.

Blue whales exist in distinct subspecies in the northern and southern Pacific. Largely solitary, they come together in groups for feeding and breeding. They have the loudest, strongest vocalizations of any animal on the planet; their calls, which consist of a series of moans and pulses, can be heard up to 1,600 kilometers (1,000 miles) away. It is thought this communication helps them find each other across vast ocean expanses.

◄ ▲ *Remarkably, the Blue whale's mind-boggling growth and gargantuan size is fueled largely by a diet of tiny, shrimp-like animals called krill, clouds of which the whales swim through, open-mouthed, to filter from the water. In the summer months the whales can ingest four tonnes (four and a half tons) or more of the protein-rich animals every day.*

The Blue whale is supremely adapted for its marine foraging: its enormous mouth is lined with fringes of tough, fingernail-like plates called baleen and its throat and belly are grooved with expandable pleats of skin. Gulping in vast quantities of krill-filled water, the whale uses its massive tongue to force the water back out through the baleen, trapping the krill in its mouth as in a net dragged from the sea.

The Blue whale

Prized by commercial whalers in the twentieth century, the Blue whale was hunted to the brink of extinction – down to as few as several hundred individuals – until it was formally protected by the International Whaling Commission in 1966. It is still regarded as endangered and scientists are uncertain how well the blue whale populations around the world are recovering. The mammal has a slow rate of reproduction, and there are concerns that the small genetic pool will hamper their ability to healthily reproduce.

Fish out of water

The remote Bikini Atoll in the Marshall Islands bears witness to a rarely observed phenomenon when the **Peppered moray eel** leaves its watery habitat to hunt for prey onshore.

Only recently documented, this land-lubbing behavior is unique to the Peppered moray, which is typically found in depths of up to 100 meters (330 feet). Just how Peppered morays adapted to the opportunity to hunt on land is unclear, but the behavior observed by the Big Pacific crew over several days was clearly not just a happy accident. At low tide, the eels venture purposefully onto the rocky shore, dipping in and out of rock pools to avoid suffocation, in search of unsuspecting crabs, which they swiftly ambush, before returning to sea. The Peppered moray also has the right equipment for the job, its strong jaws and short fangs enabling it to seize a whole crab in one go.

▲ *A Peppered moray eel leaves the safety of the sea to hunt for prey along the rocky shore of Bikini Atoll. The behavior is unprecedented and only recently documented.*

JAPAN
North Pacific Ocean
UNITED STATES
Los Angeles
HAWAI'I
⭐ Bikini Atoll
Apia
Pape'ete
AUSTRALIA

A Peppered moray eel lies in wait for a crab. Like other morays, the Peppered moray has strong, backwards-slanting teeth to prevent prey, once seized, from escaping or slipping.

Lucky break

Director of Photography Peter Kragh describes filming the Peppered moray eel hunting forays on Bikini Atoll as being the biggest 'wow' moment of the series.

The Big Pacific crew had journeyed to the remote location to film Coconut crabs and Reef sharks, but after excited scientists returned to the boat with reports of moray eels hunting on land, the film crew knew it was a golden opportunity to capture footage of the unique behavior.

Unfortunately the eels did not oblige again in that site, despite fruitless days of searching, and the crew eventually moved on to another part of the atoll. Days later the scientists returned to the boat with excitement again – but this time also with cellphone footage of the eels in action.

The next day the crew spread out along the coastline in the same spot, waiting for the eels to emerge – and they did, with fifteen eels slithering out over the algae-covered rock to hunt for crabs. The crew was lucky, it was their final day.

"We didn't have any more time, we didn't have any more chances, but we ended up getting everything we needed for a phenomenal sequence in just one afternoon," says Kragh. "It was definitely a matter of being in the right place at the right time."

▼ *The Double-crested cormorant can dive for up to thirty seconds at a time, using its wing-like flippers and strong, webbed feet to propel and steer it.*

▶ *After catching fish and the occasional crustacean in its long, hooked beak, the bird then surfaces and returns to land, where it must stand, wings outstretched, to dry off in the sun – the price it must pay for its incursion into the marine realm.*

Underwater flight

The **Double-crested cormorant** – named for two distinctive tufts on each side of its head – has evolved ideally for the demands of shallow-water diving and fishing. Its bones are proportionately heavier than those of other seabirds, it has less body fat, and its outer plumage does not repel water, instead becoming drenched after a quick dip. These are all characteristics that reduce buoyancy, helping the cormorant submerge up to several feet beneath the waves on its regular hunting forays.

A sticky end

Double-crested cormorants have become such adept swimmers that young birds may take to the water before they fly. This can be a risky endeavor, for the cormorants have a number of predators, including other seabirds.

◀ This cormorant chick perished in Californian waters, perhaps after a fall from its nest on the cliffs above. It becomes ensnared in the stinging tentacles of a Giant green sea anemone.

▼ Such accidents are happy for these anemones, which are among the largest in the world.

◀ The invertebrate slowly devours the bird's body by pulling it into the mouth located in the center of its crown.

▼ Any waste is later excreted through the same opening.

At Monterey, California Double-crested cormorant parents raise several chicks within large coastal colonies. The chicks are invariably ravenous and both parents feed them the regurgitated fishy meals on which they thrive. By ten weeks of age, the youngsters will leave the nest completely.

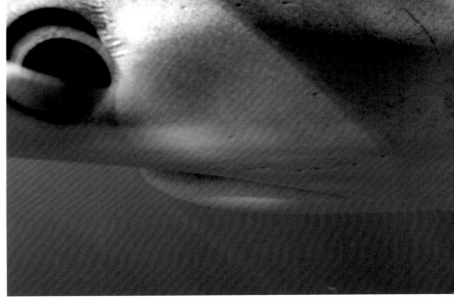

Speed machines

The **Shortfin mako** is the world's fastest shark. It has been clocked at up to 32 kilometers (20 miles) per hour and also holds the record for long distance oceanic travel – up to 58 kilometers (36 miles) per day over 2,130 kilometers (1,320 miles).

Perfectly hydrodynamic in shape, the mako also has the ability to selectively heat parts of its body temperature above that of the water. This endothermy enables it to digest food faster, stay alert and be more active in cold water than most other fish. It can also transfer energy to its muscles more effectively to achieve explosive bursts of acceleration – all ideal attributes for a lethal predator of pelagic fish species such as tuna, mackerel, swordfish and sea bass.

◀ Like a well-designed sports car, the mako has evolved for speed.

▲ ▶ Blue sharks are a pelagic species often seen in the same waters as Shortfin makos. They are easily distinguished from their faster cousins by their coloration, lean body and long snout and pectoral fins.

Making friends with mako sharks

Big Pacific's Director of Photography Mike Bhana has been diving with sharks for more than twenty years, and in that time has developed a deep understanding of their behavior – and the risks that come with meeting them face to face in their own habitat.

For Big Pacific, Bhana filmed Shortfin mako sharks off the northeastern coast of New Zealand, in a location where adolescent makos tend to congregate. He and a support diver entered the water with multiple sharks measuring up to 2 meters (7 feet) in length, using just a PVC rod or shark shield for protection.

Bhana's approach to observing and filming these predators without a cage is based on years of personal experience and documented science.

"When you get in the water with sharks, the majority will never have seen a human before, so they need to figure you out. You need them to understand that you're not prey, but you're not a challenge either – you want them to perceive you as another predator that is their equal.

"Obviously you have to focus on your job, which is to get the footage, but you also have to focus on your own behavior, and on the sharks. You can't afford to show fear, because the sharks will sense it – and they will then see you as prey."

Bhana explains that the sharks will often give a series of 'tells' – behavioral indicators of increasing agitation – to which he must be attuned and ready to react. These include closing their mouths and lowering their pectoral fins – both potential precursors to a charge or even an attack. And if a larger shark turns up, Bhana will get out of the water.

"With mako sharks there's a hierarchy based on size, and once they reach maturity the structure of that hierarchy changes. When they get to two meters (seven feet) or more in length, they're starting to target bigger prey – and that can include humans."

Like their close cousin the Great white, the mako shark is an ambush hunter, but whereas the Great white relies on stealth, the mako uses its speed.

"Typically an adult mako will approach you to check you out, circle you, and then swim out of visibility. That's when you know that they're likely to come back at you from behind – and fast – and that you need to get out of the water."

Bhana has enormous respect for mako sharks, and he applauds the widespread adoption of anti-finning legislation that is seeing a resurgence in their numbers, but he is also keen to stress a 'Don't Try This at Home' message for Big Pacific viewers and readers.

"Seeing people like me doing what we do, people can get lulled into a sense of false security about sharks, but they need to remember that these are incredibly dangerous animals. I don't recommend anyone gets in the water with sharks if they don't know what they're doing – the risks are just too great."

Graceful grazers

While many marine animals can be mesmerizing to watch underwater, few can match the balletic movements of the **manta ray**. Unfurling their wing-like fins – which can span up to 7 meters (23 feet) in the larger of the two manta species – the rays often appear to fly through the sea like migrating birds.

Like many of the Pacific's largest inhabitants, manta rays feed on some of its smallest organisms – plankton – and their graceful swoops and barrel rolls are typically associated with feeding behavior. This is when a manta opens its horn-like mouth fins as it surges through the water, effectively creating a funnel that channels water into its wide, toothless mouth. Plankton is trapped as the incoming water streams through the five feathered gill plates that line the animal's throat, and the protein-rich mixture is then flushed into the animal's stomach with a kind of coughing action.

▲ *The distinctive coloration of manta rays, including the spots on their undersides and patterning on their backs, enables individuals to be identified.*

◀ *Smaller than its pelagic cousin, the Giant oceanic manta ray, this Reef manta ray can nonetheless reach a wingspan of up to 4.5 meters (15 feet).*

▶ *Manta rays live in continual motion. Negatively buoyant, they must keep water flowing over their gills, and will slowly sink if they stop moving forward. This is because they are members of the shark family and, like all sharks, do not have swim bladders that enable them to adjust their buoyancy. Also in common with other rays and sharks is their flexible, fibrous skeleton which is half the density of bone – an energy-saving product of evolution that also contributes to their underwater elegance.*

▼ *The word 'manta' is Spanish, meaning 'cloak' or 'shawl' – an apt analogy for the distinctive diamond shape of these restless rays.*

◀ *As its name suggests, the Reef manta ray typically frequents coral reefs, tropical islands and atolls and other coastal areas, often gathering in large numbers where waters are rich in plankton to participate in an elaborate feeding 'dance'.*

Manta rays

Because of their size, adult manta rays have few predators in the wild, but their dimensions offer little protection from their newest and most dangerous predator – humans. Both manta species are considered vulnerable due to the high numbers being fished and killed by entanglement in fishing lines and nets. Manta gill rakers are also sought after for use in Chinese medicinal products. This demand is driving international trade in manta products, and international protection is required to prevent further decline in population.

Giant drifter

Another plus-sized Pacific denizen is **Nomura's jellyfish**, a gargantuan grazer that spends most of its life adrift in the Yellow and East China Seas.

Starting life as a pinhead-sized polyp, this peripatetic monster mushrooms rapidly – in less than a year – to 2 meters (6½ feet) in diameter and more than 200 kilograms (440 pounds) in weight. To fuel this extraordinary growth – up to a 10 percent increase in size per day – the juvenile jellyfish feeds on tiny plankton particles through a mouth which measures just a millimeter (3/64th inch) across.

◀ ▲ *The Nomura's jellyfish grows rapidly from this tiny size to become one of the largest jellyfish on the planet.*

▶ The Nomura's jellyfish has no eyes or brain. It can only control its depth in the water, otherwise drifting at the mercy of the currents.

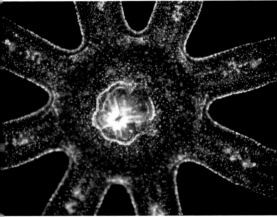

▲ The single mouth of a juvenile Nomura's jellyfish measures less than one millimeter. It will grow many hundreds of these by adulthood.

▶ The sting of the Nomura's jellyfish is not sufficiently toxic to kill a human but it is very painful and can cause a build-up of fluid in the lungs.

The ravenous appetite of the burgeoning jellyfish cannot be satisfied by one miniscule mouth, however, so as the invertebrate grows, it develops more mouths of the same size beneath its umbrella-shaped bell. Zooplankton, fish eggs and larvae are pushed up towards these mouthlets by the pulsating action of the jellyfish through the water and the movement of its grasping tentacles. An adult Nomura's jellyfish is said to be able to filter an Olympic-sized swimming pool of plankton in this manner in a single day.

Nomura's jellyfish

Once limited to the Yellow Sea, the Nomura's jellyfish is now regularly found in the Sea of Japan, where mass aggregations of the animal are causing a headache for local fishers. No one is sure why population explosions have been seen there in recent years, but scientists suspect they are linked to the rising sea temperatures associated with global warming. This could be exacerbating population outbreaks already attributed to nutrient build-ups arising from coastal and agricultural development, and to overfishing – the last because of the severe reduction in the numbers of fish species such as swordfish and tuna that prey on the jellyfish and thus help keep a check on their numbers.

The giant Nomura's jellyfish couldn't eat these small fish even if it wanted to. Its hundreds of tiny mouths can eat only microscopic food. The fish just need to be able to dodge the vicious stings.

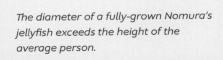
The diameter of a fully-grown Nomura's jellyfish exceeds the height of the average person.

Forest fellers

At up to 30 meters (100 feet) long, the **Giant kelp** found in the temperate coastal waters of the Pacific Ocean is popularly known as the longest 'seaweed' in the sea. But the kelp is not actually a plant at all, rather a marine algae – the world's largest – and as such does not have roots, instead clinging to its rocky anchor point with a branching structure known as a 'holdfast'.

Kelp provides habitats for thousands of marine species and creates one of the most diverse ecosystems on Earth – something like an underwater rainforest. It can grow as fast as 60 centimeters (2 feet) a day, its long 'blades' ultimately forming a canopy on the water's surface that provides important shade and shelter for the species that live beneath it. But in the cool waters off the coast of California the kelp forests – and the animals that rely on them – are under threat.

▼ ▶ *Since Giant kelp is not a plant, it does not have roots, instead using a lattice-like structure known as a 'holdfast'.*

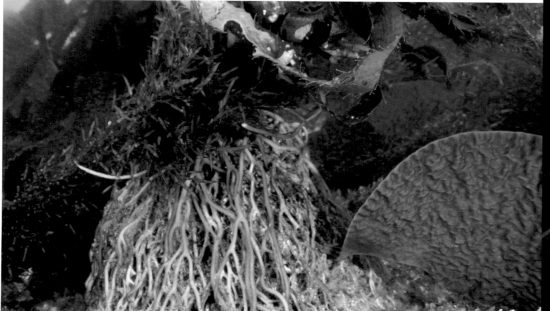

◄▲ The Red sea urchin may not look like much but they are a formidable foe to Giant kelp. They move on a thousand suckered feet, and light sensitive cells on their bodies act like rudimentary eyes. Most impressive, their teeth (seen below) can cut through stone.

◄ The Purple sea urchin is smaller than the Red sea urchin, but has the same diet and range, and predator – the Sea otter. The animals perambulate across the seafloor on their spines and tubed feet, congregate at the base of kelp and with their sharp teeth make short work of the kelp holdfasts.

The **Red sea urchin** is a spiny, bottom-dwelling invertebrate with a seemingly endless appetite for Giant kelp. It scours the seafloor, moving surprisingly quickly on tubed feet that extend through holes in its hard external skeleton. When it finds a kelp holdfast, it quickly chews through the tough, fibrous cords with its five razor-sharp teeth. Effectively sawn from its anchor, the long 'blade' of the kelp soon dies – while the urchin moves on to its next meal.

The insatiable Red sea urchins – which are the largest urchin in the world – can devastate swathes of Giant kelp forest in a matter of days. Scientists attribute the ballooning numbers of the destructive spiny grazers to the reducing population of **Sea otters**, one of the urchin's few natural predators.

With their powerful jaws and tough mouths, **Sea otters** can readily crunch through an urchin's spines and skeleton, usually attacking the urchin's underside where the spines are shortest. Until recently this natural control kept urchin numbers in check, but the Sea otter has become endangered and the resulting blow-out in urchin numbers demonstrates the delicate balance in which marine ecosystems everywhere hang.

▲ ▶ *Sea otters are the only marine mammals to pluck or catch food with their forepaws, which they do on dives lasting up to several minutes in duration. They also use rocks to pound their prey, making them the perfect foil for the prickly urchins as well as mollusks, such as abalone.*

◀ *The seemingly violent aquatic tussle of this male and female is actually a courtship that will result in mating – and perhaps also a bite wound or two for the female.*

A bonanza for bottom-dwellers

Not all ocean inhabitants are primary consumers – either a hunter or grazer. Scavengers and decomposers also play an important role in marine food webs by converting organic material into energy. In the waters off California the demise of a top predator, a Leopard shark, results in more than one meal for California Spiny lobsters over twelve days. It also feeds bacteria we can not see, and the nutrients released by these tiny animals will, in turn, feed the phytoplankton that forms the basis of the food web.

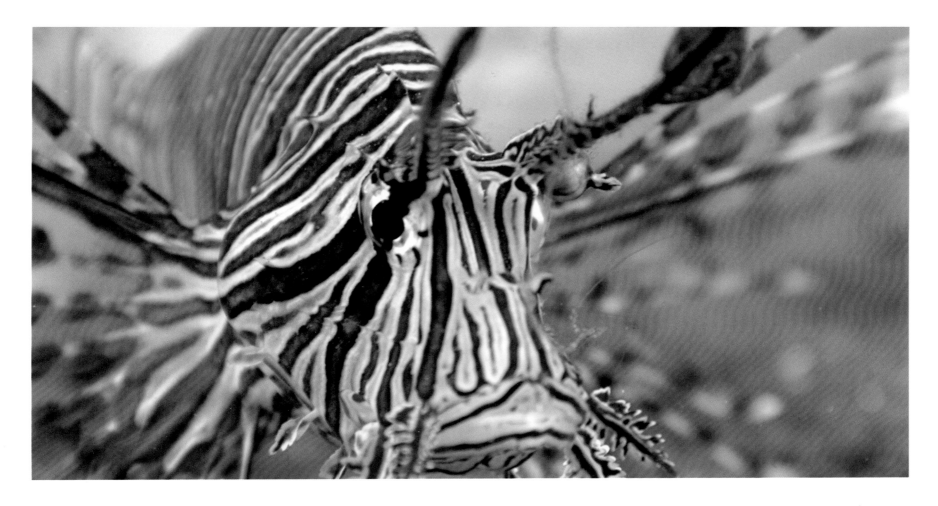

A lethal lion

True to its name, the **Red lionfish** is a carnivore best avoided by other fish and humans alike, for its spines are poisonous and its sting painful. A member of the Scorpionfish family, its venom contains a neurotoxin that affects muscular and cardiovascular systems.

A native of the South Pacific and Indian Oceans, the Red lionfish is now invading other seas, likely as the result of its release – either deliberate or accidental – from aquariums.

◄ *A lionfish's spines – twelve or thirteen of them on its dorsal fin alone – help to give it a fearsome appearance. And so they should; each is capable of delivering a nasty dose of toxin produced in glands at the spines' base.*

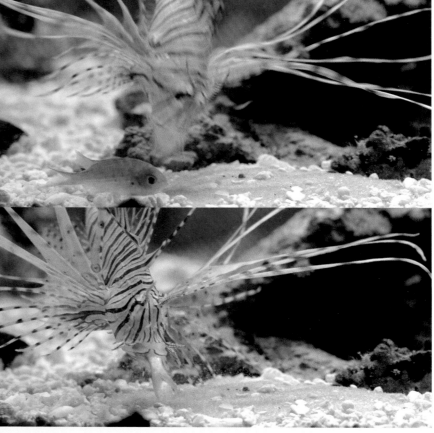

A small but deadly predator, the lionfish hunts on small fish and crustaceans. Prey are cornered and intimidated by the outstretched pectoral fins of the lionfish in full ambush mode, then ultimately snaffled in one gulp with a lightning-quick snap of the jaws. It's all over in less than 1/10th of a second.

▶ The Red lionfish grows up to 38 centimeters (15 inches) in length, but it has the courage of a much larger animal, for it is seemingly undeterred by other reef predators. It tends to be a solitary animal.

The map shows:

New Caledonia ★   FIJI

AUSTRALIA

Sydney ●

NEW ZEALAND

◄▲ Sundews are named for the sticky droplets, resembling morning dew, found on the end of their hairy tentacles.

▶ A bug comes dangerously close to death as it skirts the rim of the pitcher plant's 'pitfall trap.' If it falls in, it will eventually be converted into a solution of minerals, that help to sustain the plant in nutrient-poor soils.

Predatory plants

Separated from the ancient continent of Gondwana 100 million years or so ago, the islands of New Caledonia in the southwest Pacific are remarkable for the huge number of endemic flowering plants which have evolved in isolation since then. Among them is the **New Caledonia sundew**, one of the fastest-moving 'predators' of the plant kingdom and the **pitcher plant**.

These carnivorous plants developed an appetite for meat because they grow in nutrient-poor soils. They trap insects in the sticky hairs that grow on the end of their 'tentacles'. The hairs of the sundew are actually glands and the digestive juices they produce also help to decompose the prey. Pitcher plants, on the other hand, lure insects into a deep cavity filled with liquid. Once inside this 'pitfall trap' they cannot escape.

Intricate intruders

In an era of global shipping the price of trans-Pacific travel is often paid not by the travelers themselves but by species forced to make way for them in their newfound homes. So it is with the spread of the **fan worm**, a native of the Mediterranean Sea now residing in many harbors throughout the Pacific thanks to the 'free ride' it can catch on the countless ships and boats that constantly crisscross the world's oceans.

With its delicate, feathery tentacles the fan worm appears, at first glance, benign, but the invader is actually wreaking havoc on the Pacific harbor habitats where it takes hold, where there are often few natural defenses.

As the fan worms multiply, they form a carpet of invaders that smothers out opportunities for other organisms. By vacuuming up precious nutrients from the sea *en masse*, the introduced fan worms displace native filter feeder species such as mollusks and small fish. With a single female fan worm capable of producing more than 50,000 eggs in one season, it's easy to see how quickly the scale of an invasion can become catastrophic.

▲ *The Mediterranean fan worm is an unwelcome invader that hitches a ride on boat hulls to colonize new harbors.*

◄ The worm lives in a flexible, leathery tube and uses its 'fan' to trap planktonic particles in the water and channel them to its mouth.

◄ Once fan worms are established, it's nearly impossible to eradicate them – the only option is to physically tear them from their anchors. Broken worm segments can regenerate into new individuals, so divers must carefully bag every worm to prevent further infestation.

Roaming reptiles

Perhaps the best known Galápagos inhabitants are the tortoises after which the archipelago was named – the word 'galápago' meaning tortoise in Spanish. Sometimes weighing in excess of 400 kilograms (900 pounds), they are the world's largest tortoise, and also one of its longest lived.

Galápagos tortoises can survive without food or water for six months or more by breaking down body fat to produce sufficient water and nutrients. This remarkable adaptation helps them endure droughts on the islands' arid lowlands, but also led to their mass exploitation by whalers and sealers who captured and kept the animals on board their ships as a convenient source of fresh meat for long sea voyages. This led not just to a rapid decline in Galápagos tortoise numbers but the extinction of several sub-species once found on the islands.

MEXICO

CUBA

CENTRAL AMERICA

VENEZUELA

COLOMBIA

Galápagos Islands ⭐   • Quito

ECUADOR

▲ *Galápagos tortoises enjoy a varied diet that can include cacti, grasses, leaves, lichens, berries, melons, and other fruit – including an introduced species of guava.*

▲ ▶ *The unforgiving volcanic terrain appears to worry Galápagos tortoises little. They move regularly from arid lowlands to lusher highlands, over time creating trails across the landscape.*

Typically the herbivorous animals' diet is the product of a daily routine which sees them wander along well-worn paths from the lower slopes of their island homes to the volcanic highlands. Here the tortoises enjoy the abundance of water and plants – including an introduced and highly invasive species of guava that now seems to be sustaining some tortoise populations.

Other introduced species, however, do not have an up-side for the Galápagos tortoise. Today the remaining 20,000 individuals face challenges from predation of their eggs by rats, pigs and voracious ants. The tortoises also compete for food with introduced mammals such as goats. It is likely their ability to endure famine will assist their survival into the future as it has done in the past, but they also need protection from the introduced perils against which they have no natural defense.

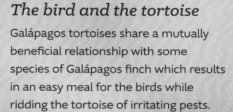

The bird and the tortoise

Galápagos tortoises share a mutually beneficial relationship with some species of Galápagos finch which results in an easy meal for the birds while ridding the tortoise of irritating pests.

The exchange is initiated by the birds, which face the tortoise and hop around with exaggerated movements. When the tortoise is ready to participate, it rises up, extending its neck and legs to enable the birds to access usually inaccessible spots on its body, such as the skin between its carapace and plastron. The birds then duck in to pick off parasites – but they must be quick, for some irascible tortoises have been known to drop down suddenly on unsuspecting birds, flattening them in one blow... and then eating them!

Darwin's finches

The Galápagos inhabitants most closely associated with Darwin are the so-called **Galápagos finches**, 'so-called' because they are not true finches, but a group of fifteen closely related but nonetheless distinct species of tanagers that can be identified largely by their different beak shapes.

When Darwin returned to England with specimens of each animal it gave science its first close look at the process of adaptive evolution in an isolated island space. In the case of the finches, each unique bill had evolved to favor a specific diet or seed. On the Galápagos, it was determined, all the birds had evolved from just one ancestor to fill different ecological niches – a perfect illustration of the process of divergence of species. The little, otherwise unremarkable birds thus became an icon for adaptive radiation – and forever linked to the man who made them famous.

◀ ▶ Evolved from birds that colonized the Galápagos perhaps two or three million years ago, Darwin's finches remain similar in plumage, mating behavior and nesting habits. Diversity in their beak size and shape, however, enables them to exploit different foods. It is thought this has proved particularly successful in terms of helping them survive in the dry season, when food becomes scarce.

Ancient mariners

With 97 percent of its reptiles and land mammals found nowhere else, the Galápagos archipelago has one of the highest levels of endemism – species unique to one place – on the planet. A prime example is the **Marine iguana**, a land-living reptile that forages underwater for marine algae and can dive more than 9 meters (30 feet) beneath the water's surface to do so.

Unsurprisingly, this lizard has evolved adaptations to equip it for this amphibious lifestyle, including long claws and strong limbs that help it cling on to the rocks in coastal currents and wave wash.

◀ *The Marine iguana of the Galápagos is the only lizard in the world that dives for its food. The post-swim sunbathing they enjoy warms their reptilian bodies, which have been chilled by the cold Galápagos waters.*

▶ *A peculiar adaptation is the iguana's ability to excrete the salt which builds up as result of the animal's sea-grazing habits. Special nasal glands filter salt from the iguana's blood. The animal then 'sneezes' it out – which explains the crusty white cap that decorates every marine iguana's head.*

Although comfortable in the cool Pacific waters of the Galápagos, the iguanas cannot remain long in the water or their body temperature will drop too low. As reptiles they rely on external heat sources, so in between dips they warm themselves by sunbathing on the rocks, their dark skin helping them soak up the equatorial sun. This period of post-swimming lethargy is when they are most vulnerable to predation, but as the iguanas are characteristically aggressive their natural predators are few.

Their main threats appear to be introduced predators such as dogs and cats, and climatic events, such as El Niño, which increase the local water temperature and impact the growth of the algae on which the iguanas rely.

▶ *Marine iguanas have adapted well to their unusual grazing habits. Their small teeth are set very close to the edge of their jaws to enable them to gnaw efficiently at the short algae, while their clawed feet provide a firm anchor against the tidal swell.*

Marine iguanas thermoregulate thier bodies. If getting too hot, the animals may push their bodies up off the dark, sun-warmed rock.

Marine iguanas are vulnerable to the effects of El Niño weather patterns, when warmer sea surface temperatures and reduced marine nutrients impact the seaweed on which they typically feed.

Island adventures

No exploration of the Big Pacific would be complete without meeting the animals that developed in the splendid isolation of the Galápagos archipelago. After more than 25 years working in the Galápagos, Director of Photography Richard Wollocombe knows the islands well, and so was the ideal person to explore them for Big Pacific. But nature has a way of confounding even close familiarity, ensuring the crew still faced challenges during their visit.

Wollocombe is a highly experienced diver and underwater camera operator, but shooting the unique underwater grazing habits of the Galápagos' Marine iguanas for Big Pacific raised a specter that he would rather not have faced again.

Wollocombe explains that the shoot entailed a visit to a popular grazing spot that is also the local 'hangout' for a 2-meter (6½-foot) female Bull shark. Wollocombe had 'met' the aggressive shark on a previous shoot, when the only thing that had saved him from its jaws had been his safety diver, who managed to ward the animal off. Naturally Wollocombe was reticent about returning to the same spot, and indeed the cantankerous shark was still patrolling the same section of coastline. Fortunately she didn't make a second attack – perhaps her curiosity had been sated, or she didn't like the taste of wetsuit – and the Big Pacific filming proceeded without interference.

A shoot on the slopes of Alcedo volcano, on Isabela Island, proved similarly unnerving, albeit for a different reason. Boasting the largest number of Galápagos tortoises, Alcedo offers the ideal location for filming their idiosyncratic foraging habits.

The tortoises doggedly climb the volcano's slopes in search of the lush vegetation that grows at higher altitudes, and the resulting images of these primordial animals passing by sulfurous, steaming fumaroles transport viewers back in time.

Alcedo is still very active, however, and it is thought the high levels of silica in its rock generate more violent eruptions than those of other Galápagos volcanoes. Its most recent eruption was in 1993, but a major eruption 100,000 years ago is known to have virtually wiped out the entire resident tortoise population.

Knowing the volcano's propensity for violence gave Wollocombe a few nerves, especially when the Big Pacific filming period coincided with a period of tremors – a known precursor of volcanic activity.

"When we arrived on the rim of the caldera I noticed a considerable increase in fumerolic activity since my last visit there in 2007. The subsequent tremors certainly added substance to my observation and fueled my imagination. It was quite unnerving to be standing on the sulfur fields, thinking they could blow at any time. Yes, there was only a miniscule chance of that happening, but had it happened, there is no way we could have escaped in time."

Despite potentially volatile conditions Isabela has been the location of encouraging conservation success. Like many Galápagos islands, Isabela has been ravaged by introduced species such as rats and pigs. An explosion in the number of feral goats in the second half of the twentieth century almost denuded it of the small trees and shrubs that tortoises rely on. A project aimed at eradicating the pests was launched in the 1990s and by 2002 had succeeded in ridding the island of the problematic goats, sparking a resurgence in the vegetation that constitutes much of the tortoises' diet.

The Galápagos Islands

Straddling the equator some 900 kilometers (563 miles) from the coast of Ecuador, the Galápagos are a group of volcanic islands best known for their association with the theory of evolution. The naturalist Charles Darwin's visit there, in 1835, helped him develop ideas about natural selection and contributed to a field of science that altered not just our understanding of evolution but the way humans saw their own relationship with the world.

Nearly two centuries on from Darwin's visit, the archipelago is grappling with the consequences of its fame and widespread fascination with its unique wildlife. Annual visitor numbers, growing year on year, reached an all-time high of 215,691 in 2014. Ironically, the resulting pressure on both land and marine resources is threatening the very environment and wildlife that tourists come to see. Local fauna is falling victim to a variety of human impacts, from vehicle collisions to introduced viruses, while water and land pollution degrades once pristine habitats. The Mangrove finch, one of the species which so inspired Charles Darwin, has dwindled to around 100 individuals. It's hard to imagine what he might have to say about this.

But people and their by-products aren't the only hazard; with human visitors come an army of unintended invaders. Mammals such as rats, pigs and goats, first introduced to the islands by whalers two centuries ago, are still creating conservation challenges; in modern times it is invertebrates such as ants and marine organisms, hitchhiking a ride on boats and planes, that threaten the fragile Galápagos ecosystem. Just how the balance between economic development and environmental protection will be managed into the future is uncertain, but one thing is clear – the Galápagos Islands ecology needs our help if it is to survive.

In the arid or semi-arid conditions on some of the islands of the Galápagos vegetation can be limited to plants such as the prickly pear cactus, a favorite food for Galápagos tortoises.

Leviathan

The **Whale shark** has captured popular imagination ever since the Norwegian explorer Thor Heyerdahl made the species famous on his epic Pacific journey on the *Kon-Tiki* raft. Named for its size – it is the world's largest fish – the Whale shark cruises the temperate and tropical waters of all of the world's oceans, but is most commonly found in warm waters where upwellings deliver rich pickings of plankton.

Like their distant cousins the manta rays, Whale sharks are filter feeders. They spend most of their time near the sea surface, moving through the water with their toothless maw open wide. In this way a Whale shark is capable of filtering up to 6,000 liters (1,585 gallons) of water an hour, taking plankton, krill and small fish from the water as it passes through their gill rakers, which act like a sieve.

Whale sharks are perhaps the ultimate Pacific wanderer. Tracked individuals have travelled thousands of miles across great tracts of ocean. Little is known of their life cycle, however, including how long they live, how quickly they reach maturity, or where they reproduce. They are likely to be both slow-growing and slow to reproduce. For this reason they have been classed as 'Vulnerable', particularly given the threat of unsustainable fishing in Asian markets where their fins are in high demand for shark fin soup.

◄ ▲ *Reaching up to 12 meters (50 feet) in length, Whale sharks are readily identified by their blue-gray dappled skin, ridged body and large dorsal fin.*

*Ocean is more ancient than the mountains,
and freighted with the memories and the
dreams of Time.* — H. P. LOVECRAFT

Mysterious
Pacific

We yearn to unravel the mysteries of the Pacific.
But she does not give up her secrets so willingly.

IT IS AN OFTEN-CITED AXIOM that we know more about the surface of Mars than we do about the depths of the ocean, the vast majority of which remains off-limits to us. Instead we must settle for the glimpses into an alien world that we dredge up in fishing nets or capture in startling light with remotely operated vehicles – strange creatures as unknown to us as the place they came from.

We must wait for the Pacific to reveal its mysteries to us. The incredible artistry of the pufferfish is one such closely-guarded secret, only just exposed; the hidden existence of the glass sponge, another. There are many questions still to be answered. How do turtles navigate with such pinpoint accuracy across both sea and time? On what chance of nature did the horseshoe crab survive the events that extinguished so many other species? And what did ancient peoples know of the sea and its inhabitants – perhaps something from which we could learn?

We would do well to remember that the ocean is the evolutionary cradle from which our distant ancestors first crawled from millions of years ago. Although we may now consider ourselves masters of that watery universe that birthed not just us but all life, we still have much to learn from it, and our tenure on Earth grows ever more tenuous the more we ignore our impact on the ocean.

The truth is we humans are merely scratching at the surface of the Big Pacific. Beneath its waves, an ocean of secrets awaits us.

◄ *The sheer rock column that creates Malpelo Island, 500 kilometers (310 miles) west of Colombia, plunges down to the Malpelo ridge. The island's waters are a gathering place for hammerhead sharks and so are popular with divers.*

A turtle tide

In Costa Rica's rainy season, usually around the start of the quarter moon, one of the Earth's most extraordinary natural phenomena takes place on a beach in the northwest of the country – the *arribada* or 'arrival' of the **Olive ridley turtle**.

No one knows *what* constitutes the mysterious call that urges hundreds of thousands of female turtles to come together at this one time, some from thousands of miles away. Perhaps the lunar cycle drives their journey, perhaps they respond to the internal impetus of hormones.

What we do know is *how* the turtles respond; amassing offshore until the time is right, then making their exodus from the sea to sandy shore.

▶ *Turtle* arribadas *occur at only a few locations worldwide when female Olive ridley turtles return to the beach where they themselves hatched, perhaps ten years earlier. How they retrace the thread of their oceanic wanderings back to this one place is a mystery still to be answered.*
Perhaps clues lie in water chemistry, or the Earth's magnetic field.

HONDURAS
EL SALVADOR
NICARAGUA
Caribbean Sea
COSTA RICA
Ostional ★
PANAMA

▶ The Olive ridley – named for the color of its heart-shaped top shell, or carapace – is the smallest of sea turtles. It grows up to 65 centimeters (2 feet) in shell length and weighs up to 45 kilograms (100 pounds). Olive ridley turtles are omnivorous. They can dive up to depths of about 150 meters (500 feet) to feed on a variety of food that includes algae, seaweed, mollusks, crustaceans and fish.

▲▶ The turtles dig shallow nests in the beach sand and deposit their soft-shelled eggs. Those laid in the first two days of the arribada have little chance of hatching, as they are often dug up by turtles that follow.

Often exhausted by their oceanic odyssey, the turtles crawl up the beach and, at around the high tide mark – it is thought they smell the intensity of the salt in the sand to determine the right spot – begin to dig in the sand with their rear flippers. Into these excavations they each lay a clutch of around one hundred eggs, then cover them over before laboring back to the sea, often battling through hordes of incoming turtles on the way.

Early clutches often fall victim to those that follow, for latecomer turtles can't avoid digging up other eggs already buried in the beach. At Ostional Wildlife Reserve the event is also eagerly awaited by a host of predators, including Black vultures, and feral dogs, which consume the eggs with voracious gusto.

Around fifty days later, the same predators will line up in readiness for a different kind of arrival: the hatching of eggs that survived the tumultuous turtle stampede, scavenger hunt and human harvest.

The infant turtles run another kind of gauntlet, even more heart-rending than that endured by their mothers. For as the tiny turtles crawl towards the sea, as mysteriously driven to its embrace as their mothers were impelled to leave it, they are picked off by dogs, vultures and seabirds all over again. Once in the open ocean, predators such as large fish and sharks await them. Little wonder that the survival rate of eggs to adulthood is estimated at just one in one hundred.

◄ *The instinct of hatchling turtles to head for the sea is as mysterious as their mothers' keen sense of direction for their nesting beach, but they must run a gauntlet of predators first, and others await them in the ocean.*

▶ At Ostional Wildlife Reserve local people can legally harvest the Olive ridley eggs for both commercial sale and their own consumption. Although contentious, the practice is regulated and some of its proceeds pay for beach and turtle protection. Hundreds of thousands of eggs are taken, but only those laid in the first two or three days of the *arribada*, for studies suggest the likelihood of those eggs hatching is much lower compared to those laid later.

Turtle tomb

Several species of sea turtle are seen in the waters around Sipadan Island in Malaysia, but deep beneath the island itself is a different concentration of turtles – a labyrinthine limestone cave in which the remains of many of the marine reptiles lie in tomb-like repose. Exactly how the turtles ended up in the cave is unknown, although it is likely the animals were simply unable to find their way out.

Turtle beach

Witnessing Costa Rica's turtle *arribada* had been on Scott Snider's personal 'wish list' for many years when the opportunity to film it presented itself as part of the Big Pacific project. And while the scale and drama of this event did not disappoint, the director of photography wasn't necessarily prepared for the emotional impact of the experience.

Snider is active in turtle protection in his home state of South Carolina. In Costa Rica, after seeing the female Olive ridley turtles' heroic struggle to reach the beach, clamber onshore – often over each other – dig in the sand and deposit their eggs, Snider was understandably unsettled by the amount of predation the eggs then incurred.

Local people have gathered to collect the eggs at Ostional Wildlife Reserve for decades. Research suggests that clutches laid in the first two days of the *arribada* have little chance of hatching, so gathering the eggs during this time is sanctioned – the only place in Costa Rica where the egg harvesting is legal. Even so, Snider struggled to reconcile himself to the sheer scale of the harvest, which numbers in the hundreds of thousands of eggs.

"As a person raised to fight to save every turtle nest in America and many other places around the world, it was hard to watch the human harvest even if the science says it's okay," says Snider.

More difficult to stomach were the local and feral dogs who dug hungrily in the sand, devouring any egg they uncovered and destroying others in the process. These predators are a relatively recent addition to the list of species that line up to benefit from the turtle bonanza. In turn, their excavations expose more eggs to other opportunists, the Black vultures. The birds are longstanding natural predators, but until recently were only able to access eggs uncovered by the action of turtles. The dogs effectively increase the extent of the birds' natural predation because they expose more nests.

"It's fair to say that predation is quite high when an *arribada* is completely natural and wild too," says Snider. "That said, watching domestic animals eating hundreds of eggs and hatchlings is unacceptable and it was all I could do not to interfere. I had to remember that it's my job to document what's happening. It's better to stand back, get the images and tell that story than it would be to fend off a dozen dogs. The story can be told in a stronger way by bringing back compelling images."

Sea turtle

All seven species of sea turtle face serious threats and populations around the world have drastically declined in recent times. This is likely due to a combination of illegal hunting, habitat degradation, and the high numbers killed in fishing nets. Sea turtles are protected in many jurisdictions, but a black market still exists for their shell, skin and eggs. Females are particularly vulnerable when nesting, and egg poaching is a widespread problem. Relatively inexpensive modifications, such as the introduction of Turtle Excluder Devices – openings that allow turtles to escape – can make many fishing nets a lot safer for turtles and drastically reduce the by-catch toll.

Living fossils

First appearing in the fossil record about 550 million years ago, the **Chambered nautilus** is the only survivor of a group of chamber-shelled cephalopods called ammonites. It is also related to octopus, squid and cuttlefish, but is the only one to still wear a hard external shell.

'Cephalopod' means 'head-foot', to describe animals whose feet – or, in this case, tentacles – are attached directly to their head. The Chambered nautilus has around ninety small tentacles. Unlike the tentacles of octopus and squid these do not have suckers, instead relying on a series of grooves and ridges to grip prey and hang on to the rocks, along which they pull themselves when not swimming.

The Chambered nautilus eats small crustaceans and fish and also scavenges on dead animals. It tends to be found near the seafloor or coral reefs, at depths of up to 500 meters (1,650 feet). Its many-chambered shell – as many as thirty – is the secret of its ability to stay upright and control its buoyancy, which it does by releasing gas through a tube that runs through the center of the chambers.

The ancient **ammonite** is one of a large number of fossils found throughout the world. The animals disappeared during the mass extinction event around 66 million years ago, likely to have been the result of a large comet or asteroid impact, which wiped out 75 percent of the world's plant and animal species. Mysteriously, the nautilus was the only ammonite to survive this cataclysm. One possible reason lies in its reproductive strategy, for the Chambered nautilus lays its eggs throughout its lifespan in small batches near the seafloor, where it also feeds on a range of small organisms. Other ammonites, it is thought, were filter feeders that laid just one large slew of eggs at the end of their life in the open ocean. These then formed part of the planktonic mass near the ocean's surface. The nautilus was thus doubly protected from the deadly consequence of the impact. The lengthy winter killed the plankton that had been both the ammonite's food source and its nursery, while the nautilus was still able to feed and continue its breeding, relatively unaffected.

▲ *A fossil relative of the Chambered nautilus, the ammonite was once found throughout the world's oceans.*

◀ *The Chambered nautilus has only primitive eyes without any cornea or lens. It is thought that it relies primarily on its sense of smell to detect prey, and on its sense of touch to detect obstacles in the water.*

Horseshoe shore

The **horseshoe crab** is a mysterious remnant of the past, a survivor whose evolution predates the dinosaurs, and even flowering plants. Like the nautilus, it survived the mass extinction event that claimed so many other organisms. There are just four species worldwide, and together they claim their very own taxonomic class in the pantheon of modern day Animalia.

Horseshoe crabs are not really crabs at all, and in fact are more closely related to spiders and scorpions than the crustaceans with which we commonly associate them. Like crabs, they have an exoskeleton or shell, but unlike crabs

their shells are made of chitin and protein rather than calcium. A juvenile horseshoe crab will shed its shell five or six times in the first year of its life alone; it takes about seven years for it to reach its adult size.

Chinese horseshoe crabs are found in the western Pacific, especially along the coast of China and Japan. During the breeding season, adult crabs move from deeper to warmer, inshore waters. Here the female lays between 60,000 and 120,000 eggs in several batches, which she buries in sandy beaches. The male, clinging to her back, fertilizes the eggs at the same time.

▲ *Chinese horseshoe crabs have six pairs of jointed legs. Their body is divided into three parts: a head and thorax section, a smaller abdomen section and a tail, which enables it to flip its body if it is turned upside down.*

Chinese horseshoe crab

In an ironic twist of fate the ultimate example of evolutionary resilience now faces its toughest survival test. Pollution, overfishing and habitat destruction are all contributing to serious population decline for the Chinese horseshoe crab, despite it being granted protection in Japanese waters in 1928. In an effort to support the species, researchers at City University of Hong Kong foster young horseshoe crabs through their most vulnerable lifestages from larvae through to juvenile age. Schoolchildren also get involved by helping release young horseshoe crabs into the wild. It is hoped that, through the program, they will become advocates for the species and help to safeguard its future.

Once hatched the larvae remain in these nests throughout the winter, sustained by the yolks in their egg sacs. Come summer the juveniles remain buried in the sediment at high tide, but emerge at low tide to scour the exposed sand and mudflats for small shellfish, worms and algae. Only when adult do the crabs head to deeper waters.

The horseshoe crab's reliance on coastal habitats not just for breeding but also the development of juveniles makes the crabs doubly vulnerable to the widespread development taking an environmental toll on Pacific coastlines. The survival rate of a horseshoe crab in its first year is estimated to be only one in 10,000. Declining populations are also making it difficult for breeding partners to find each other in inshore waters.

▲ *Researchers at City University of Hong Kong help foster young horseshoe crabs from the egg to juvenile stage to increase survival rates during this vulnerable period of the animal's lives.*

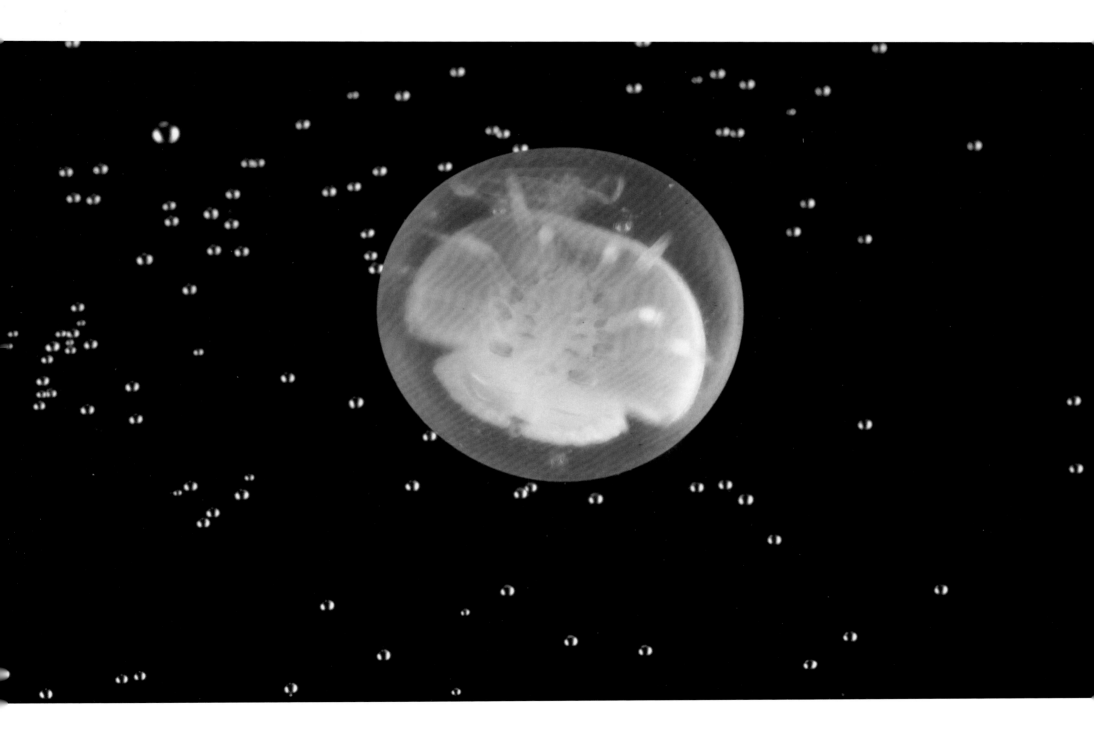

Creatures of the coast

A resident of the seas between southern China and northern Australia, the **Chinese white dolphin** is a coastal-dwelling cetacean with some unique traits.

Calves are born dark gray, but the animals' skin grows increasingly lighter with age. By adulthood some populations are nearly white, while others take on a distinctly pink hue – perhaps due to the overdevelopment of blood vessels near the surface of their skin. No one knows why this adaptation has proven successful for the marine mammals, which live in murky coastal waters, river deltas and estuaries.

Unlike many of their pelagic cousins, Chinese white dolphins are moderately slow swimmers that only frequent shallow waters. They are, however, plucky and have been known to chase off and even kill sharks. They typically live in pods of ten or fewer individuals in which females only become sexually mature at around ten years of age, and only bear calves every three or so years. This means their populations are slow to regenerate – an important factor in their overall resilience to the many perils they now face.

◄ Adult Chinese white dolphins are white or pink, but the animals are born dark gray and their skin color changes as they mature – hence the gray hue of two of the dolphins seen here.

Chinese white dolphin

Chinese white dolphins are rapidly diminishing in number due to the burgeoning coastal development – including land reclamation, large construction projects and pollution – impacting their habitat. Fishing is another threat, as the dolphins can become entangled in nets. Escalating shipping activity increases the risk of physical collision, while the noise from marine traffic and construction activity interferes with the dolphins' ability to hunt and communicate. Populations such as the few groups remaining in Hong Kong waters and along the west coast of Taiwan are considered critically endangered, and will likely become extinct unless strong protection measures are put in place.

The Lazarus lobster

In the 1700s, when Europeans first landed on Lord Howe Island, 600 kilometers (370 miles) from the eastern coast of Australia, they were amazed at the large, flightless insect they found there. Officially they called it the **Lord Howe stick insect**, but it came to be known colloquially as a 'tree lobster' simply on account of its impressive size – up to 12 centimeters (5 inches) for females.

In 1918 rats were accidentally introduced to the island, and the tree lobster population was wiped out within two years. That, it seemed, was that for the Lord Howe stick insect. Fast forward eighty years, however, and a surprising and hopeful discovery was made by chance on Ball's Pyramid, an inhospitable volcanic islet 23 kilometers (13 miles) away from Lord Howe island: a small population of Lord Howe stick insects, with twenty-four individuals found alive and well on just a single bush.

◄ *The Lord Howe stick insect evolved in isolation on Lord Howe Island without mammalian predators. Not only was it able to fill an ecological niche occupied in many other parts of the world by mammals, it was able to assume its giant proportions. Its size, slow gait and flightlessness did not present a problem – until the arrival of rats.*

Like the much larger Lord Howe Island, Ball's Pyramid is the remnant of an ancient volcano. It stands taller than the Empire State Building and stretches, sheer-faced, from the sea rather like a basalt iceberg. There are no trees on the exposed outcrop, only a single type of shrub along with some grasses, and indeed the entire Lord Howe stick insect population there is limited to a patch of just 180 square meters (1,938 square feet) where there is sufficient moisture and shelter on the otherwise rocky, bare island.

The find was a lucky one. The small population has enabled a captive breeding program which has led to the reintroduction of the species in its original home. But the questions of just how the flightless insect found its way across thirteen miles of open ocean to Ball's Pyramid remains unanswered.

It's possible the original population could have floated there on a raft of vegetation, although the travelers would then have had to scale the sheer rock face to reach the one and only location where they could survive. Perhaps seabirds carried individual insects there over a period of time. A more intriguing possibility is that some of the insects, which were once used for bait by local fishermen, somehow escaped from their hook and found a sanctuary on the Pyramid. The secret will likely remain the Big Pacific's forever.

▲ *Following the discovery of the Ball's Pyramid population, two mating pairs of the Lord Howe stick insect were collected there for a captive breeding program. The insect has since been re-introduced to its original home.*

▶ Lord Howe stick insect juveniles are bright green, and become darker with age as they molt. They are typically nocturnal animals and are solely herbivorous.

Perfect circles

The incredible industry of the **White spotted pufferfish** is an example of the wonders even now still revealing themselves in the Big Pacific.

The story begins in 1995 when divers noticed delicate circular patterns, up to 2 meters (6½ feet) in diameter, in the seabed off the coast of Japan. Like crop circles, these geometric patterns appeared mysteriously – or perhaps miraculously – and perfectly formed, with round, intricately crenellated centers surrounded by a series of sculpted, radially aligned peaks and furrows.

Scientists were baffled until, in 2013, their creator was observed to be a small, otherwise unremarkable pufferfish, later deemed a new species. This unassuming artist represents one of nature's most appealing examples of paternal nesting behavior, for the immaculate sand circles prove to be all-important in determining a female's selection of a mate.

▲ *At around 7 or 8 centimeters (3 inches) in length, the White spotted pufferfish is dwarfed by the scale of its handiwork, which can be up to 25 times its size in diameter.*

Appreciating underwater artistry

A highlight of Big Pacific for Director of Photography Peter Kragh was the opportunity to film a newly discovered species of pufferfish off the coast of Japan.

Only a year or two prior was the White spotted pufferfish revealed as the creator of the intricate circular structures seen on the seafloor, and its remarkable building behavior had been captured by filmmakers just once. Kragh and his colleague Ernie Kovacs saw an opportunity to capture it in a way not often done underwater – in a perfectly static shot from directly overhead – to show the nest's perfect symmetry to best advantage.

"We could have just held a camera above a nest site," explains Kragh, "but underwater you can never be completely still. A perfectly static underwater camera shot has a different quality, and that's what we wanted to achieve."

The pair's solution was to build a large tripod that they then positioned over several pufferfish nest sites to get the ultimate shot. The resulting images have an almost ethereal quality – a fitting tribute to the artistry of this remarkable fish.

Males carve out their submarine works of art over the course of a week or more through a combination of fanning with their fins, burrowing with their bodies and shoveling with part of their lower jaw. Here and there they may even add a small flourish, such as a shell or small stone.

The fish are as fastidious in the maintenance of their circle as they are in its creation, carefully removing in their mouths any marine debris that threatens to mar the aesthetics. They must also be vigilant in protecting it from the effects of the shifting tides, and so constantly work to re-define its peaks and contours with busy ministrations.

Scientists speculate that a nest's appeal to a potential mate lies in its superior design and pleasing presentation. When a female pays a visit to the circle's outer rim, the male stirs up the sand in the center of the circle, perhaps to demonstrate its fine grade. If the female is interested she enters the circle and the male makes feints at her by rushing in from its outer perimeter. The center is where a female – if she so obliges – will lay her eggs, which are fertilized by the male as he bites her mouth repeatedly. The female then plays no part in the eggs' care, leaving this chore to the male, which flaps its fins to stir the eggs and also drives away any would-be predators.

▲ *Male White spotted pufferfish are methodical in their artistic endeavors, energetically burrowing in the sand to create the radial furrows of their circles, and adding ornaments or removing offending objects.*

Sacred site

In a corner of Micronesia the ancient stone city of **Nan Madol** is a megalithic complex constructed – literally – out of the Pacific Ocean. The mysterious remains of a powerful political dynasty and place of important religious rituals, it consists of a network of more than 90 artificial islets built up from a coral reef and topped with massive basalt structures. Just how 750,000 tonnes (827,000 tons) of stone were transported to the site and placed without pulleys or levers of any kind is a mystery, as is the purpose of the canal network that links the island complex together.

Archaeologists believe the people of Pohnpei Island began building up the islets with stone and coral as early as 500AD. Later – likely between the twelfth and thirteenth centuries, around the same time as structures like the Cathedral of Notre-Dame in Paris or the temples of Angkor Wat in Cambodia were being built – immense stone walls and buildings were added. As many as 1,000 people lived in the city at its peak, when it appears to have been a well-organized metropolis in which different areas were set aside for specific activities, such as canoe-building and food preparation.

◀ ▲ It is not known exactly when the basalt construction began at Nan Madol, but the builders would have to have transported the large pieces of rock from quarries in distant parts of Pohnpei island.

The city was the seat of the island's rulers. The king or *saudeleur* resided in the city center along with other nobles, enclosed within a high wall. Other areas were reserved for religious ceremonies. On the islet known as Idehd, a sea turtle was sacrificed each year to 'the great spirit ' – a sacred eel kept in a pool there.

Eels held a special place in Nan Madol culture and the canal network that links the 75-hectare (185-acre) complex may have been the way in which the animals entered into and moved throughout the city. Certainly oral traditions suggest this. Indeed the name Nan Madol means 'spaces between' – perhaps an indication of the cultural significance of these watery byways.

The majesty of Nan Madol is thought to have endured for 1,000 years until the city and its rulers were routed by a competing clan around 1500AD. It was abandoned soon after. Today it serves as an evocative reminder of Micronesia's rich cultural past and a rare example of a megalithic built environment in the Pacific region.

▲ *The foundations of Nan Madol were constructed of basalt boulders on top of which longer pieces of rock were built up in a 'header and stretcher' pattern. The resulting walls could have reached up to 15 meters (49 feet) in height and 5 meters (16 feet) in thickness.*

◄ *Eels are still considered sacred in parts of Micronesia. The freshwater eels seen here being fed by Pohnpei islanders are found near one of the quarries where the basalt rock was mined for the construction of Nan Madol.*

Boulder beauty

At Moeraki beach on New Zealand's South Island a curious array of perfectly spherical rocks resemble giant marbles. To the indigenous Māori people, these represent eel baskets cast from the nearby wreck of an ancestral canoe. But to geologists they are the result of ancient forces – concretions of hard rock that formed within the seabed sixty million years ago. Over time these were eroded from the softer mudstone that surrounded them to lie exposed on the beach. Others can be seen in nearby cliff faces.

▲ *Moeraki boulders can measure up to 3.6 meters (12 feet) in circumference and weigh several tons. The 'veins' that run across their surface are filled with yellow calcite.*

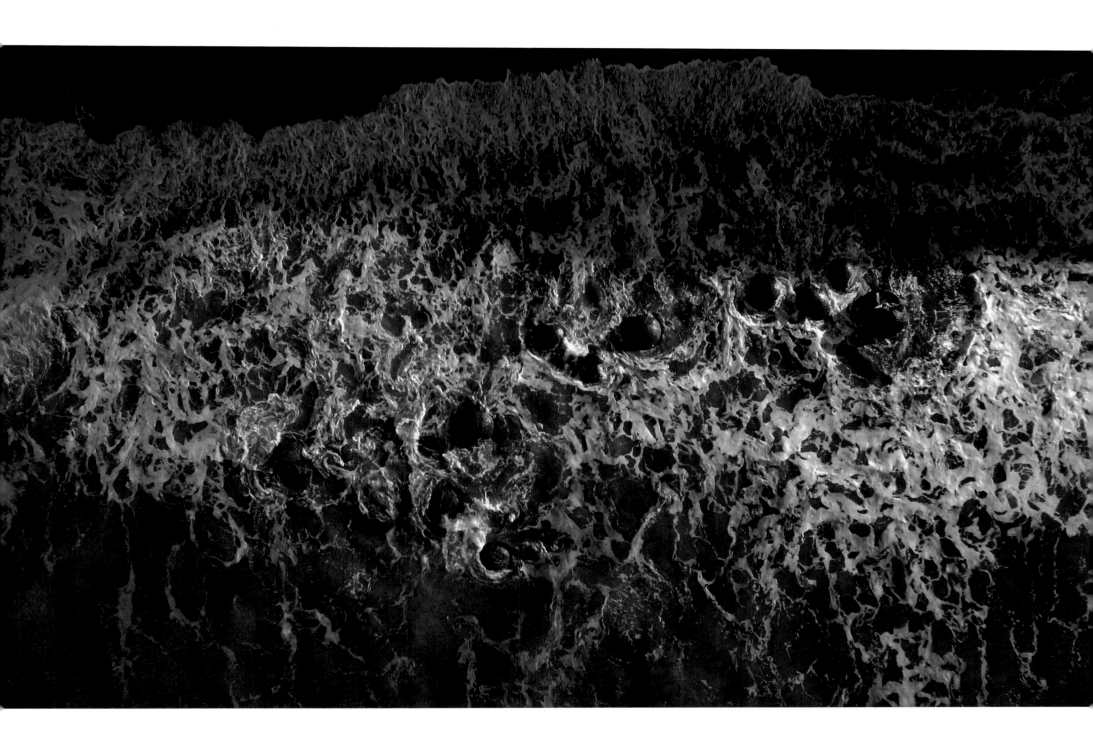

Sea of Japan

Toyama Bay

SOUTH
KOREA

● *Nagano*

● *Tokyo*

JAPAN

◀ *A female Firefly squid releases her eggs into the shallows. The eggs will float on the ocean tides, as part of the sea's planktonic soup. The female, her job done, will soon die.*

Light show

For several nights every spring the waters off the coast of Japan are alight with a dense display of bioluminescence. This is the **Firefly squid** or *hotaru-ika*, an elusive deep-water dweller that amasses in inshore waters just once a year for a spectacular spawning event.

The small squid – they grow to just 7 or 8 centimeters (3 inches) in length – typically live at depths of several hundred feet but rise to the surface at night to feed on tiny crustaceans. However, they must travel to shallow inshore waters to release their eggs. Here the female squid gather in their millions, providing a bumper – albeit brief – opportunity for local fishers, for they will die soon after spawning.

▶ *The Firefly squid's bioluminescence is a rare type produced by tiny, light-emitting organs called photophores dotted throughout the squid's body. These can be lit up either in unison or in alternating patterns to lure prey, frighten predators, or attract a mate. The light show also serves as camouflage, for the squid is able to match the brightness and color of its underside to light coming from above, making it difficult for predators to detect it from beneath when it is feeding near the water's surface.*

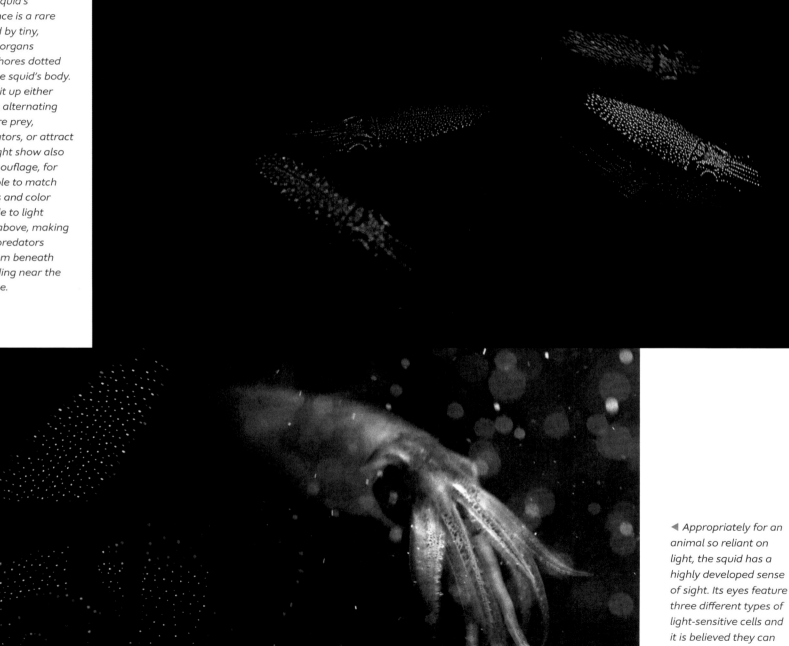

◀ *Appropriately for an animal so reliant on light, the squid has a highly developed sense of sight. Its eyes feature three different types of light-sensitive cells and it is believed they can distinguish colors.*

From tide to table

Several tons of Firefly squid are caught every year by commercial fishers in Japan, where the squid is considered a delicacy. Despite the large annual harvest and the fact little is known about the species' population, the fishery is considered sustainable.

The twilight zone

The shorelines and blue-green shallows are what we humans tend to imagine when we think of the ocean, because we often encounter this accessible realm – or even live by it. The vast majority of the Big Pacific, however, is a shadowy, watery continent still waiting to be explored, and its many secrets remain hidden to us air-breathing land-dwellers.

The primary challenge facing pioneers of 'the twilight zone' – the mid-sea depths between 200 and 1,000 meters (660–3,300 feet) – and the inky abyss below it are the unforgiving laws of physics. At sea level we are subject to one atmosphere of pressure – equivalent to around 15 pounds per square inch – but every 10 meters (33 feet) of depth adds another atmosphere of pressure. A depth of 900 meters (3,000 feet) equates to 1,500 pounds of bone-crushing force from every direction – obviously unsurvivable for humans and only recently within the range of super-strong, impeccably designed submersible vehicles.

Such technology now enables us to begin to explore what is the largest ecosystem on Earth, an alien world of light-emitting animals and gentle-moving giants. The denizens of the deep are supremely adapted to life in low temperatures, high pressure, little or no light and a relative paucity of food. We are only just beginning to fathom the mysteries of their survival. Perhaps the answers will one day assist us with our own, as we move into a future shaped not by natural forces, but those of our own making.

◀▲ *Sixteen years in the making, Nuytco Research's Exosuit can dive to depths of 300 meters (1,000 feet) while keeping the diver at one atmosphere of pressure. It combines sufficient rigidity to withstand the outside pressure with the flexibility required for movement. Its link to the surface is a 380-meter (1,250-foot) umbilical cord.*

◀ *This glass sponge reef is estimated to date back 9,000 years, yet it is extremely fragile, and will shatter with the slightest of touches.*

Glass carpets

Until the late 1980s the prehistoric glass sponge reef was relegated to fossildom, a Mesozoic-era marine phenomenon that had existed once upon a time, in once instance covering a 7,000-kilometer (4,350-mile) swathe of ancient ocean. So the discovery of the continued existence of glass sponge reefs in depths off the western coast of Canada, in 1986, rocked the scientific world.

The glass sponge may look like a plant but it is actually an animal, and the world's oldest multi-cell organism. Over time the sponges form vast reefs that sustain complex marine communities. Growing on top of each other and on the skeletons of their forbears, these statuesque structures can reach up to eight stories in height.

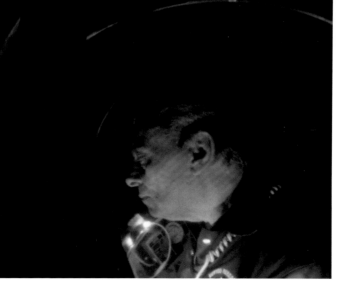

◀ *British Columbia-based engineer, inventor and explorer Dr Phil Nuytten dives in his home waters near Vancouver. Over the years, Phil and his team at Nuytco Research have created a fleet of submersibles and work with NASA and other scientific organizations.*

▲ *Nuytco's submersibles are designed so that the pilot is always at one atmosphere. One of the submarines is Deep Worker, a single-pilot vehicle that can dive up to 1,000 meters (3,300 feet) below the surface.*

These are the times of dreamy quietude, when beholding the tranquil beauty and brilliancy of the ocean's skin, one forgets the tiger heart that pants beneath it; and would not willingly remember, that this velvet paw but conceals a remorseless fang. — Herman Melville

Violent
Pacific

This ocean is the epicenter of natural mayhem... where the Earth is crushed into dangerous landscapes and inhospitable environments.

CONTRARY TO THE NAME, *el Mar Pacífico*, given to it by Ferdinand Magellan, the Pacific can be anything but a peaceful sea. The birthplace of typhoons and volcanoes, a battleground for fierce animal contests and, more recently, a backdrop to devastating human-borne destruction, it is as much an ocean of brute force and fearsome aggression as one of tranquility and calm.

Often this violence is an integral part of the circle of life, for it is a fundamental law of nature that only the strongest survive. Whether feeding, breeding, simply surviving or dying, the lives that play out across the Pacific region are all in some way characterized by competition. Such everyday struggles have helped create the Pacific's dazzling diversity of life – and death – over millennia.

Into these existential hunting grounds and battlefields, we humans have arrived as – at best – peaceful observers or – at worst – destructive interlopers. The ultimate hunter and deadliest destroyer, we hold the fate of even the fiercest Pacific predator in our hands. Researchers are trying to determine whether the Big Pacific is resilient enough to endure the new and often terrible forms of violence we visit upon it, so that its inhabitants may continue to fight their own battles for survival, as nature intended, well into the future.

▶ *White Island, off the coast of New Zealand, shakes and rumbles as cracks in the surface blast hot gas into the air, leaving behind toxic sulfur deposits.*

Ring of Fire

Ironically, the ocean once named for its beguilingly peaceful demeanor lies within a volatile geological cauldron known as the Ring of Fire.

The Ring of Fire is the result of plate tectonics – the movement of huge slabs of the Earth's crust, called plates, that fit together to form a constantly moving jigsaw puzzle. Collision points between plates often create geologically active zones. The Ring of Fire represents the least stable part of our Earth's crust, a horseshoe-shaped area where the giant Pacific Plate rubs against its neighbors.

About 90 percent of all earthquakes occur along the Ring of Fire, and all but three of the 25 largest volcanic eruptions of the last 12,000 years have originated among the many hundreds of volcanoes dotted around its edges, which represent three-quarters of all volcanoes on the planet.

Ghostly remains

This violent history has left many marks on the Pacific coastline, particularly in the Pacific Northwest, where a fault area known as the Cascadia subduction zone stretches from Northern California to Vancouver Island in British Columbia.

The fault is the result of tectonic forces that are pushing the Pacific's oceanic crust beneath the continental North American plate. This creates an unstable zone subject to frequent tremors and devastating volcanic eruptions, such as the 1982 eruption of Mount St. Helens in Oregon.

In 1700 a massive earthquake in the Cascadia zone caused the coastline to sink up to 3 meters (10 feet) in a matter of seconds – a cataclysm which claimed this sunken forest. Careful analysis of the growth rings of these tree 'specters' has revealed that they were killed by the sudden inundation of salt water that followed this seismic upheaval. Scientists later discovered that the same event gave rise to a monster tsunami that battered Japan approximately ten hours later.

◀ *These coastal sentinels are a stark reminder of the Pacific Northwest's violent past. Submerged by an earthquake in 1700, the trees rapidly died, but their remains provide data for geologists researching activity in the Cascadia subduction zone.*

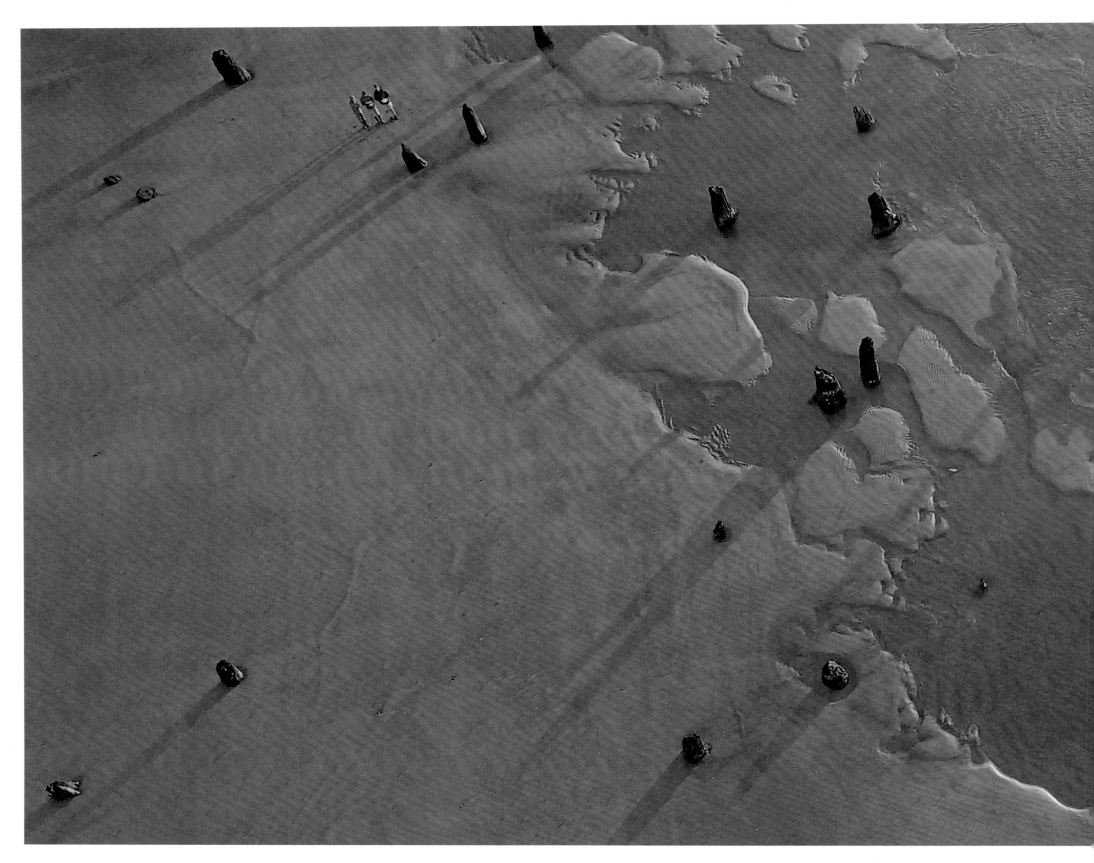

These ghostly stumps are all that remains of a once-vibrant coastal forest of spruce and cedar.

Islands of fire

Some of the islands sprinkled across the vast expanse of the Pacific originate from so-called 'hot spots' beneath the Ring of Fire. These are areas where heat rises from deep within the Earth, melting rock below the crust. The molten rock then pushes through cracks in the crust, forming volcanoes. Some of these remain beneath the ocean while others emerge as islands. The Hawai'ian islands – actually a chain of volcanoes of which some remain submerged – are one example. Kueishantao Island – also known as Turtle Mountain Island – is another.

The southernmost of a string of volcanic islands off the eastern coast of Taiwan, Turtle Mountain has been the site of dramatic eruptions; eighteenth-century accounts record bright red lava flowing from a massive schism in its cone. It also features constellations of submarine fumaroles and

solfataras – hydrothermal vents in the sea wall and floor which spew hot, sulfuric water and toxic gases into the sea.

These ongoing eruptions create an acidic environment incompatible with most forms of life. **Sulfur vent crabs**, however, have adapted to this 'no-man's-land' and are able to neutralize the sulfuric acid. Living in dense clusters inside the vents themselves, the crabs feed on zooplankton – tiny crustaceans, fish larvae and mollusks – which die in the deadly waters and sink down to the seafloor in an eerie snowfall.

◀◀ *Ongoing underwater eruptions at Kueishantao Island are visible on the sea surface as milky stains.*

▲ *Remarkably, Sulfur vent crabs have adapted to life in the vents and subsist on the 'snow' of zooplankton which dies in the acidic seawater.*

SOUTH KOREA

JAPAN

• *Shanghai*

CHINA

Kueishantao Island

Taipei • ★
TAIWAN

Philippine Sea

Forces of nature

▲ Named for the white cloud in which it is constantly enveloped, White Island is an active volcano off the coast of New Zealand.

Other Pacific islands are born of the titanic tussle between tectonic plates as they jostle against each other. The main islands of New Zealand are one example. They sit astride the edges of the Pacific and Australian plates, and their mountainous landscape, seismic activity and thermal hot spots are all testimony to the constant tug of war going on beneath their feet.

Nearly 50 kilometers (30 miles) from the country's northeastern coast, these forces are visible in the shape of a living, breathing, grumbling volcano. Named 'White Island' by Captain James Cook in 1769 for the cloud of white steam in which it was constantly shrouded, the island is actually the summit of a much larger underwater volcano that climbs 1,600 meters (5,249 feet) from the seafloor. It remains highly active, with multiple eruptions recorded in recent history.

◀ White Island's environment is extremely sulfuric. Sulfur crystals form at the many vents where steam and hot gases are released into the air, while the volcano's crater lake is acidic enough to strip flesh from bone.

▼ The island's streams are home to extremophiles – primitive but tough microbes that thrive in conditions hostile to normal life.

◀ In the late nineteenth and early twentieth century, miners worked the island's sulfur deposits and built a factory on the crater's floor. One described the island as "the worst hell on Earth – a place where rocks exploded, where teeth went black if they weren't cleaned three times a day, and where the land shook violently." In 1914 part of the crater wall collapsed killing eleven men.

Storm warning

The warm waters of the tropics may appear benign, but when mixed with the right atmospheric and weather conditions they can give rise to ferocious storms in which winds spiral at speeds in excess of 140 kilometers (85 miles) an hour. In the western Pacific these are called 'typhoons', while in the eastern Pacific – as in the Atlantic – they are known as hurricanes.

Typhoons and hurricanes form over tropical seas when warm water temperatures create disturbances in air pressure. Areas of high-pressure air start to move towards areas of low pressure, where the winds begin to spin and gain in strength. This spiraling is driven by the Earth's rotation; in the northern hemisphere typhoons spiral in a counter-clockwise direction, and in the southern hemisphere, a clockwise direction.

These meteorological monsters cut swathes of devastation along their paths, which can be notoriously difficult to predict. Their ferocity is measured by the Saffir-Simpson scale, on which a Category 1 storm has the lowest wind speed and a Category 5, the highest.

▲◀ Although picture-postcard-perfect most of the time, the warm waters of the tropics can also power devastating typhoons and hurricnaes.

Mobile home hunters

An Okinawa beach buried in trash in the wake of a typhoon is a bonanza for **Blueberry hermit crabs**. Usually nocturnal, these opportunistic scavengers emerge in the aftermath of Pacific storms to comb the coastline for windfalls, such as an easy meal or new home. Brightly-hued plastic containers are particularly popular with these crustaceans, which are able to distinguish color, and the crabs' adoption of them gives new meaning to the term 'recycling'.

Pelagic plastic

The amount of debris seen here is a sobering indication of the inestimable volume of plastic now awash in the Pacific. Pelagic plastic, much of which comprises tiny particles suspended in the water, comes from land-based sources as well as marine pollution, such as the dumping of fishing nets. The debris is then ferried by wind and currents into remote stretches of the North and South Pacific Ocean, where it forms gyres or large patches. No one knows definitively how large these concentrations are – but the cost of plastic pollution on marine animals such as seabirds and whales, often found with stomachs full of plastic, is well-documented.

War zone

▲ ▶ A World War Two relic rests beneath the waves off the coast of New Guinea. It is thought the Japanese pilot landed the plane intentionally, perhaps after becoming lost or running out of fuel.

Following Japan's attack on the American naval base at Pearl Harbor, Hawai'i, in December 1941 the Pacific Ocean became a dramatic theater of war – an arena for fierce naval battles, secret submarine missions and air skirmishes.

One relic of these violent times now rests peacefully below the waves above which it once wreaked havoc. This 'Mitsubishi Zero' – the same type of plane as used at Pearl Harbor – was likely landed at sea off the coast of New Guinea after its pilot became lost and ran out of fuel.

The Zero, or 'Zeke', was an exceptionally agile and speedy fighter plane. Between 1937 and 1945 the Japanese built 11,500 of these aircraft and they became the plane of choice for Japan's notorious 'kamikaze' suicide pilots – young volunteers who would fly their planes directly into enemy ships.

This plane, however, was destined for a different future. The small cockpit in which its pilot once guided the aircraft towards a controlled sea landing has found new life as a marine community. Eventually it will be claimed entirely by the sea, becoming a plane-shaped reef of coral and sponges, giving life in exchange for those it may once have taken.

Plane sailing

Filming a World War Two relic on the seafloor is more of a challenge than you might think, particularly if you want to show the variety of colorful life that it now supports. Colors disappear the deeper you go underwater as the available light diminishes, so at a depth of 17 meters (56 feet) the plane wreck and reef-like community it now supports would appear mainly blue and green rather than the vibrant palette it actually is.

The solution is to introduce some artificial light which is, again, not as easy as it sounds. Camera-mounted lights tend to dazzle the immediate foreground in an obvious cone of light that quickly falls off at the edges. Achieving a more natural look depends on being able to securely position multiple light sources further away from the camera. But managing this on a limited timeframe when your filming location is in a remote part of Papua New Guinea takes some serious planning.

Fortunately Big Pacific Director of Photography Peter Kragh was already well steeped in such underwater problem-solving when this conundrum presented itself. Transporting an aluminum lighting rig halfway around the world was not an option, so he knew they would need to build one on location. After ascertaining that there was a bamboo grove close to the filming location, Peter knew his solution would be to utilize the available resources.

Pieces of the bamboo were pre-cut to Kragh's specifications, and then assembled into a frame. This enabled him to mount several battery-powered lights and position them up to 8 meters (26 feet) from the camera. The resulting innovation was not just environment-friendly, it helped reveal the poignant remnants of a particularly violent period in the Pacific region and the resurgence of life that followed it.

◀ ▲ *The Skull caves of the Milne Bay area in Papua New Guinea are a sobering reminder of both the violent clashes and important cultural practices of the area's past.*

Head-hunting

In the remote Milne Bay province of Papua New Guinea a number of caves reveal a grisly secret – hundreds of human skulls neatly piled, some even glistening with an encrustation of minerals.

For many centuries coastal tribes in this area practiced exocannibalism, cooking and consuming the flesh of vanquished enemies, believing that this would pass on to them the strength and power of their foes. Some claim that the sequestered skulls are the gruesome trophies of these headhunting days. Other sources attribute the skulls to local burial rites in which the head of the deceased, once separated from the body, was placed in the cave as a mark of respect.

Grave site

The Marshall Islands are a scattering of atolls and islands spread over 925,000 square kilometers (357,000 square miles) of Northern Pacific ocean. Among their northern reaches is Bikini Atoll, the site of the United States' nuclear testing program between 1946 and 1958.

Twenty-three nuclear tests were conducted at Bikini, including the detonation on 1 March 1954 of a 15-megatonne (16½-megaton) hydrogen bomb 1,000 times more powerful than that dropped on Hiroshima. The massive explosion effectively vaporized three islands, created a mile-wide crater in Bikini's reef, and spread radioactive mist as far away as Australia and Japan. It remains the largest bomb ever detonated by the United States.

◄▲ *Remnants of massive nuclear explosions still dot the islands of Bikini Atoll.*

▲ *Radioactive isotopes build up in the tissue of corals. Scientists are testing coral samples to understand whether these long-lived animals have been affected at a genetic level.*

▶ *Tawny nurse sharks typically have two dorsal fins, but some of the population at Bikini Atoll only have one. Is this the result of genetic aberration that can be linked to the atomic testing?*

The entire Bikini area was heavily polluted by radioactive ash as a result of the testing and the atoll remains unsafe for human habitation. The soil – and anything that grows in it – is affected with high levels of Caesium 137, a cancer-causing isotope. The atoll's many Coconut crabs are among the unwitting victims of this contamination as they forage on local coconuts and pandanus, oblivious to the isotope that builds up in their bodies.

While Bikini's reef appears healthy, with a resurgence in coral growth, the range of species is dramatically reduced and scientists have noted physiological aberrations, such as missing dorsal fins in the resident Tawny nurse shark population. Whether this is due to the effects of radiation is unclear, but the long-term legacy of exposure to high levels of radiation in plant and animals species remains to be seen.

◄ *Bikini's blasted lagoon, which is visible from space, is a grave for decommissioned World War Two ships, brought in as part of the testing program. On land these abandoned bunker-like structures are the only visible remains of the testing program – but its invisible traces are everywhere.*

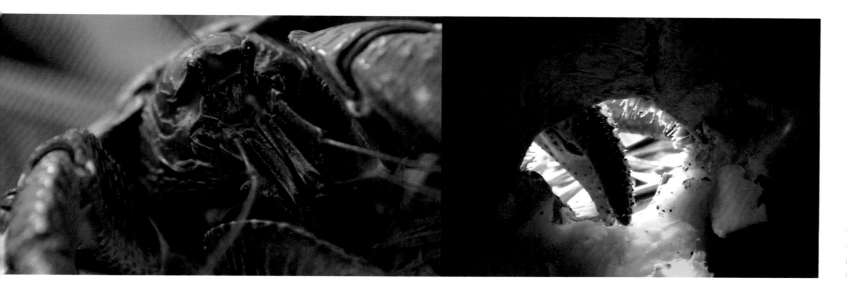

◀ *A Coconut crab's claws are stupendously strong – the mightiest by far of any crustacean and recently revealed to be almost as strong as a lion's bone-shattering bite.*

▼ *Scientists are still unsure about the effects the high levels of Caesium 137 might have on Bikini Atoll's Coconut crabs.*

The tree-climbing nut-cracker

Actually a type of hermit crab, the **Coconut crab** eschews its shell-bearing habit while still a youngster. It relies on its own carapace instead, an adaptation that enables it to exceed other crabs in size – for it has been documented at an impressive size of 1 metre (3⅓ feet) from toe to toe.

Also unlike most of its cousins, the Coconut crab has become almost entirely terrestrial, and in fact drowns if submerged in water. While its gills have adapted to breathe air, they must still remain moist. The crab achieves this by dipping its legs in water and running them over its breathing organs. The crab also returns to the sea to lay its eggs, standing in the water and casting them adrift on the tide.

Coconut crabs actually scale coconut palms if pickings on the ground are scarce. Here they are able to pinch coconuts off with their exceptionally powerful claws. Then, back down on land, the crabs peel back the husk, pierce the coconut with one of their pointed legs and enlarge the hole by breaking off pieces of the shell until they can reach the soft inner flesh.

Crafty camera work

When Big Pacific Producer John Cullum arrived on Bikini Atoll, he had his fingers crossed about seeing a Coconut crab or two. But while the crabs can be a little shy, he needn't have worried, for the minute the crew cracked open a coconut on a tiny island that is part of the atoll, more than a dozen of the giant arthropods – effectively the size of small dogs – emerged from the undergrowth, likely lured by the whiff of an easy meal.

Cullum and his crew came prepared, with two GoPro cameras and some ideas for filming techniques to try. One camera they inserted into the end of a coconut, affixing the camera so the lens pointed into it. This enabled the crew to film quintessential coconut crab behavior – the scooping out of the contents of a coconut – from a coconut's point of view. The second camera they succeeded in mounting on to the shell of one of the crustaceans. The resulting 'Crab Cam' shots are an innovative addition to Big Pacific and provide insight into the quirky crustacean's land-lubbing habits.

Courtship contests

Humpback whales seem for the most part to be mild-mannered mammals, gliding gracefully through azure tropical seas and singing haunting, ethereal songs. Come mating season, however, male Humpbacks reveal an aggressive side to their nature, pitching themselves physically against other suitors to compete for a female's favor in what is widely regarded as the biggest – literally – courtship battle in the world.

At between 12 and 15 meters long (40 to 50 feet) the male Humpbacks are typically smaller than the females they are vying for, but weighing in at up to 36 tonnes (40 tons) they still carry some serious clout. Two, three or more males engage in these highly physical contests known as 'heat runs' when they begin to chase a female. The suitors blast bubbles into the water in antagonistic challenge, thrash their tail flukes, strike each other with their distinctive, long pectoral fins, ram each other with their whole bodies and have even been known to breach out of the water and land on each other – and all while moving along at 30 kilometers (18 miles) or more an hour.

The victor of this vicious competition will mate with the female before the whales set off on their migration to summer feeding grounds in the far north and south of the Pacific. The calves are born eleven to twelve months later, when the whales have returned to the warm tropical waters where they first bred.

Despite weighing one ton and measuring 4.5 meters (15 feet) at birth, Humpback calves face many risks during the annual migration to winter feeding grounds in tropical seas such as those around the islands of Hawai'i and Tonga.

◀ *The long pectoral fins of Humpback whales give added maneuverability in the water – but they also prove a potent weapon in the violent 'heat runs' undertaken by males.*

Two Humpback whale males compete for a female in a 'heat run'. Moving through the water at speed, they swipe at each other with their pectoral fins and tails and swim into each other. The winner of the contest will mate with the female.

► *Nearly 20 percent of all calves die during their first trip, many falling prey to Orca — the Humpback whale's only known predator other than humans.*

▶ Humpbacks are baleen whales, which means they eat plankton, krill and small fish which they sieve from the sea through hair-like plates that line their enormous mouths. Indeed they are masters of filter feeding, frequently utilizing techniques that concentrate their waterborne food into bigger, tastier mouthfuls. They do this by releasing a 'net' of bubbles while circling the prey in a slowly ascending circle towards the water's surface. This practice is also performed in groups, with the collaborators even taking on different roles.

◀ Circles of bubbles on the surface give away the animals' approach from the depths; on surfacing the team of whales can then be seen gorging themselves on their cleverly corralled feast like these whales in their summer feeding grounds in southeast Alaska.

Humpback whales

A tendency to frequent coastal waters and predictable migratory routes made Humpbacks highly vulnerable to whalers from the early nineteenth century onwards. As a result their population worldwide was decimated, to between 5 and 10 percent of its original number, before commercial whaling was largely banned in 1964. Today Humpback numbers have made an encouraging recovery, although some populations are still officially classified as endangered.

Roaming reptiles

From South East Asia to Australia, the Saltwater crocodile is one of the Pacific's most fearsome predators. An ambush hunter, it typically hides in the brackish water it favors with just its eyes and nostrils above the surface, waiting for unsuspecting prey to venture too close. It then lunges forward to grab the animal with powerful jaws capable of killing even quite large mammals with one bone-crushing crunch.

Saltwater crocodiles are even hostile towards their own species, and instances of cannibalism have been widely documented. Dominant adults will also aggressively drive younger crocodiles out of their range, forcing the exiles to search for a new home. This can, at times, lead to surprisingly lengthy maritime voyages; individuals have been tracked on journeys of up to 1,000 kilometers (620 miles). During these forays a Saltwater crocodile will move with the prevailing currents and tides.

Like all reptiles Saltwater crocodiles must control their body temperature, and they do this largely by entering the water to cool down or sunbathing to warm up. This is when they can be seen lying on the banks of tidal estuaries and mangrove forests.

▲ ▶ *The Saltwater crocodile boasts a suite of impressive adaptations to its aquatic lifestyle. It has a long, powerful tail to propel it through the water, webbed hind feet, and its eyes, nose and ears are all located on top of its head, enabling it to remain virtually invisible while otherwise submerged. Salt-excreting glands on its tongue provide it with a high tolerance for saltwater. It also has a special valve at the back of its throat which enables it to open its mouth underwater without water entering the throat.*

◀ The Saltwater crocodile is the largest reptile in the world. Undocumented reports have claimed individuals as long as 8 to 10 meters (26 to 32 feet) but most commonly they reach a size of 5 to 6 meters (16 to 19 feet) and weigh in at around 900 kilograms (2,000 pounds).

▶ Apart from being hunted by humans – the Saltwater crocodile's skin is the most commercially valuable of any crocodilian's – the Saltwater crocodile has no predator other than itself. This old warlord's hide bears the scars of battles with other crocs; one day it will be beaten – and maybe even eaten – by a challenger.

▶ Saltwater crocodiles can rest underwater for up to two hours at a time or doze off in 'unihemispheric sleep' – an adaptation in which one half of the brain sleeps while the other remains alert.

Warning signs

Sidling up to a Saltwater crocodile in the open ocean was all part of a day's work for Big Pacific Director of Photography Peter Kragh. He needed to illustrate the animals' oceanic excursions – and the best way to do that was to get in the water with them, rather than filming from a boat.

The US-based Kragh had considerable experience diving with sharks, but little with crocodiles, so he did his homework. This included speaking to colleagues that had dived with and filmed American alligators, to get an idea of how the large predatory reptiles behave in the water. Then it was a matter of getting in the water, with a 32-kilogram (70-pound) camera in front and a safety diver behind him, and approaching the animals slowly.

"We filmed three different crocodiles and they each had different behaviors," says Kragh. "A smaller one was very aggressive and would swipe at the camera without warning; the biggest one was much more confident and gave more signs before anything would happen, as if it knew it wasn't worth getting bothered about things too soon. But if you didn't back off then the mouth would open, showing its teeth, and its legs would come down, and then the toes would spread out. That was a pretty clear signal to say 'back off or else' and I got out of the way."

PHILIPPINES

Philippine Sea

Lembeh Island

SULAWESI

INDONESIA

PAPUA

Banda Sea

Ambush alley

Competition for resources can force evolution in unexpected directions. In Indonesia's Lembeh Strait, a narrow strip of water between the islands of Sulawesi and Lembeh, a cast of unusual characters displays some extraordinary adaptations aimed at giving them the upper hand in their everyday battle for life and death.

▲ *Seemingly devoid of life, Lembeh Strait is a hotspot of biodiversity, where predation and avoidance are the name of the game.*

Froglike foe

The **frogfish** is obviously named, not least because of its unusual pectoral and pelvic fins, which bend like legs. These give it the resemblance of the amphibious animal to which it has no real connection, and also enable it to clamber across the seafloor in a most unfishlike manner.

The frogfish is also a cunning user of camouflage, over time changing its color to mimic its surroundings. This skill enables it to blend in alongside its neighbors – which can be coral, sponges, stones, shellfish or spiny sea urchins, depending on the species of frogfish. Completing the disguise is a lure, a worm or anemone lookalike that dangles on the end of an antenna protruding from the top of the frogfish's head. All it then needs to do is wait for a hapless fish or shrimp to happen by. Then the frogfish makes its masterfully simple but also fateful move: a sudden opening of its mouth, which sucks the victim into it in milliseconds with the incoming surge of water.

Spiny disguise

The **Urchin-carrying crab** carts its camouflage around with it. The eight-legged arthropod uses two pairs of legs to take the load, and its other two pairs for locomotion. The various species of spiny urchins ferried around in this manner afford the crab protection from predators, while benefitting from a free ride to potential new feeding grounds.

Lying in wait

Another species that ambushes its prey using concealment and disguise is the **Crocodile flathead fish**, which buries itself in loose sand or stones on the seafloor. Its dappled coloration enables it to blend in perfectly with its surroundings – only its eyes and large wide mouth are visible as it waits for its prey, in much the same way as its reptilian namesake.

Hidden hunter

At up to 6 meters (20 feet) in length, the Bobbit worm is one of the world's longest worms – and fiercest. Indeed it is perhaps hard to believe these ferocious predators are related to the harmless earthworm.

The worm's mouthparts (in the photo at right) comprise a retractable, spring-like jaw with two, scissor-like serrated plates capable of slicing its prey in half. It also injects a toxin into its victim, stunning or killing it. This enables the Bobbit worm to devour prey much larger than itself.

Bobbit worms live, head up, in burrows beneath the seafloor, with only their alien-looking appendages protruding above the sand or coral rubble. Equipped with light and chemical receptors, these antennae-like structures alert the worm to nearby prey. The worm then lunges up and out of its lair, grabs the prey with its powerful mandibles and drags it down beneath the seafloor, all with lightning speed. So fast, in fact, the worm and its prey seemingly disappears.

Viper territory

Shedao Island, in the Yellow Sea, likely became isolated from China's Liaodong Peninsula around 12,000 years ago, when sea levels rose at the end of the last Ice Age. This geographic seclusion has helped give rise to a unique species – the **Shedao Island pit viper**, a highly poisonous apex predator which is perfectly adapted to the island's unique conditions.

The snake lends the place its western name – Snake Island – for the tiny islet, which measures just three-quarters of a square kilometer (under a third of a square mile), is literally teeming with these reptiles. Indeed their population density has been estimated at one every square meter (10 square feet).

◀ *After months of waiting, a Shedao Island pit viper anticipates its next meal with the arrival of migrating songbirds.*

Map labels: • *Beijing* · NORTH KOREA · Sea of Japan · Shedao Island · SOUTH KOREA · JAPAN · Yellow Sea · CHINA

Shedao pit vipers grow up to 60 or 70 centimeters (24 to 27 inches) in length but are capable of consuming prey considerably larger than themselves as their jaws can open nearly 180 degrees. The victim of a successful strike is quickly immobilized by the snake's venom, which is injected from fangs located in the back of the snake's mouth.

This extraordinary concentration of snakes is able to survive on what is effectively just a handkerchief-sized piece of land thanks to the animals' remarkable adaptation to seasonal food sources. Twice a year, in spring and autumn, migrating birds stop to rest at Shedao en route to and from their summer breeding grounds in Siberia. These two six-week periods of plenty are the only time the adult snakes emerge from the rocky crevices where they otherwise slumber for the rest of the year; two narrow windows of opportunity on which the snakes depend for their sustenance.

Expertly camouflaged against tree branches and undergrowth, the snakes lie in wait – sometimes even on top of each other – for unsuspecting birds to land. When one alights nearby, the viper's move is swift and deadly, for its venom is highly toxic. The snake may take several days to digest its feathered meal, but this does not stop it from looking for the next one.

▲ *Shedao island is formed by uplifted sedimentary rock, and this has created the ideal environment for the snakes, its many rocky fissures affording them protection from temperature extremes during the long months in between meals.*

Shedao pit viper

Having evolved in isolation for approximately 12,000 years, the Shedao pit viper colony is unique to its island home. Scientists estimate that the population numbers 20,000 individuals at any one time, but consider it vulnerable to localized events caused by climate change, such as typhoons and droughts.

Snake central

Filming on an island literally packed full of venomous vipers is all in a day's work for Big Pacific Director of Photography Scott Snider – almost. Hailing from South Carolina, itself home to several species of viper, Snider had filmed a lot of 'fangs' in the course of his career – but the opportunity to capture viper predation in the wild was an exceptionally rare one that was too good an opportunity to pass up, even if it meant being marooned for up to 10 days in a place where the snakes occur in the greatest concentration on Earth. Needless to say Snider took extra special care with every step.

Just one bite from one of the hemotoxic snakes would have necessitated an emergency medical evacuation – neither of which events the crew was keen on experiencing. Fortunately the shoot went without incident, helped in no small measure by the snake-proof, concrete bunker-like structure in which the crew were accommodated.

Despite the remarkable numbers of snakes, Snider recalls the challenge he faced capturing their ambush behavior on camera – the obvious problem being not knowing where and when a migrating bird would land. Long hours were spent in hides identifying and filming snakes in anticipation of a grab. The crew succeeded in filming a number of snakes enjoying meals after they had nabbed a bird, but the 'money shot' eluded them.

Finally, on the second-to-last day, Snider's patience was rewarded with a spectacular sequence of a Shedao pit viper lunging for – and landing – its lunch (see following pages). It made the long, nerve-wracking wait 100 percent worthwhile.

A Shedao pit viper in action. A combination of patience and speed results in a meal for this viper – who will quickly consume the bird and hunt again, making the most of the brief bounty of migrating birds.

The Silver Dragon

One little known feature of the Pacific's wilder side is the **Silver Dragon**, the local name for what is actually the world's largest tidal bore, that occurs on the Qiantang River near the city of Hangzhou, China.

Tidal bores are natural phenomena that can occur when an incoming spring tide rushes into a funnel-shaped bay into which a relatively shallow river empties. Other factors, such the river's water level and prevailing wind direction, also play a role in determining the strength of the bore on any given tide.

The result is a huge wall of water that rushes inland from the sea. In the case of the Silver Dragon, this wave can measure up to 9 meters (30 feet) in height and travel up to 40 kilometers per hour (25 miles per hour). Its roar can be heard long before it arrives.

Over the centuries this Silver Dragon has proven deadly to both sailors and citizens; it is little wonder that the world's oldest tide table relates to the Qiantang River.

▲ ▶ *The calm waters of the Qiantang River belie the sudden violence created by the world's largest tidal bore.*

Riding the dragon

Notorious for its unpredictability, the Silver Dragon has claimed several lives in the twenty-first century alone, so chasing it wasn't without its share of trepidation for Big Pacific Director of Photography Scott Snider. He admits not knowing what to expect before he arrived on the assignment – how big could this dragon really be?

Snider also remembers that the most challenging aspect of the shoot was anticipating where the dragon might meet one of the many sea walls aimed at protecting the city and its people from the titanic surge of water. This would result in a spectacular display of its force that would best illustrate the scale of the phenomenon.

Snider was not disappointed, encountering what he describes as a "solid mass of water coming at us in a rush." Meanwhile, as he sped from location to location in a race against time for the best place to film the wave, some hardy – or perhaps foolhardy – surfers tried their luck at riding what is widely considered to be the most unusual wave in the surfing world. The upshot is some dramatic footage of a phenomenon that has been the subject of local mythology for centuries – and is now part of popular culture too.

Index